T0290020

"*Coaching for Well-Being, Productivity, and Innovation* provides a framework for self-discovery and continual improvement that moves beyond just setting goals. Dr. Bengtson's process will help you break through stagnation and leverage your preferences and motivations to achieve your most important life goals."

Dawn M. Johnson, *Assistant Professor, The College of St. Scholastica, USA*

"I highly recommend Dr. Bengtson's book as a go-to guide for busy professionals interested in optimizing well-being, purpose, and passion."

Stacy Johnston, *Founder, AudacityHR, USA*

Coaching for Well-Being, Productivity, and Innovation

This book presents Perception Coaching® as a model that enables coaches to support their clients in understanding the impact of their attitudes in themselves, helping individuals, teams, and organizations reduce their inherent biases to more effectively collaborate, innovate, and support each other.

Dr. Bengtson approaches coaching through the lens of educational psychology in three parts, starting with understanding self and others, moving on to interactions and teams, and finally culture and organizations. Filled with strategies throughout, the book focuses on examining natural patterns of thinking and acting to uncover perceptual filters so that the unexamined and unexplained may be brought to light and understood. Covering topics such as emotional intelligence and communication styles, the book aims to help coaches support their clients pursue purpose, increase inclusion, and create innovation.

This book is invaluable reading for current and aspiring coaches and non-profit and corporate leaders, as well as talent development professionals.

Barbara J. Bengtson, PhD, is a research-informed professional development specialist with over 20 years of experience. She is the developer of Perception Coaching® and is also a performance and career coach based in the USA.

Coaching for Well-Being, Productivity, and Innovation

Using Perception Coaching with Individuals, Teams, and Organizations

BARBARA J. BENGTSON

Routledge
Taylor & Francis Group

NEW YORK AND LONDON

Designed cover image: nopparit@ Getty Images

First published 2024
by Routledge
605 Third Avenue, New York, NY 10158

and by Routledge
4 Park Square, Milton Park, Abingdon, Oxon, OX14 4RN

Routledge is an imprint of the Taylor & Francis Group, an informa business

Library of Congress Cataloging-in-Publication Data
Names: Bengtson, Barbara J., author.
Title: Coaching for wellbeing, productivity, and innovation : using
perception coaching with individuals, teams, and organizations / Barbara
J. Bengtson.
Description: New York, NY : Routledge, 2024. | Includes bibliographical
references and index.
Identifiers: LCCN 2023023311 (print) | LCCN 2023023312 (ebook) | ISBN
9781032365862 (hbk) | ISBN 9781032365855 (pbk) | ISBN 9781003332770
(ebk)
Subjects: LCSH: Personal coaching. | Organizational effectiveness. | Teams
in the workplace.
Classification: LCC BF637.P36 B46 2024 (print) | LCC BF637.P36 (ebook) |
DDC 158.3--dc23/eng/20230822
LC record available at https://lccn.loc.gov/2023023311
LC ebook record available at https://lccn.loc.gov/2023023312

ISBN: 9781032365862 (hbk)
ISBN: 9781032365855 (pbk)
ISBN: 9781003332770 (ebk)

DOI: 10.4324/9781003332770

Typeset in Avenir and Dante
by KnowledgeWorks Global Ltd.

Contents

Preface and acknowledgements

The coaching profession is adding members and growing at a tremendous rate as are the tools available to coaches. So why one more approach? The pandemic, economic uncertainty, and divisive rhetoric have culminated in creating strange ambiguities regarding certainty, science, and differences. The core of Perception Coaching® is talent development grounded in the belief that everyone has extraordinary talent which can be made visible to the world. Not only that, talents and efforts directed at prosocial behaviors have the potential to improve the lives of everyone. When differences are seen as strengths, respect is the norm, and individuals are free to live authentically, society can break down the barriers created by the challenges it faces.

Perception Coaching® starts by recognizing the preferences individuals have and works to expand the limits to understanding to increase their ability to navigate life with well-being, purpose, and optimism. This additional approach in the expansive library of coaching resources provides a unique tool for actively supporting others using prosocial attitudes. Each tool out there meets a specific need for specific people; the goal of Perception Coaching® is to provide space, strategies, and perspectives so that clients are more resilient in the face of challenge and willing to expend effort to overcome barriers.

Coaching is a practice improved by relationships, both personal and professional. It is difficult to trace interactions that spark ideas, suggest theories, provide proof of concept evidence, and bolster mood and energy. I would like to recognize many of those who supported my efforts: Mark Ziebarth, Susan Burris, Tanya Warmka Siedlecki, Anne Johnson, Brad Windschill, Krisanne Wessel, Lisa W. Byrne, Judi Maddox, Barbara Curnow, Bill, Louise, Macy Curnow and their respective families, Joanne Batterberry, Erin Wojciechowski,

Alex Campanini, Steven Stern, Joenah Sisson, Barb Luke, Danielle Armbruster, Amy Ugstad, Michelle Maki, Charlotte Blair, Steven Bucks, Claudia Cottrell, Sandi Larson, Judy Breuer, Laura Ness, Naomi Christenson, Maureen Plaunt, Michelle DeNoble, Christopher Correia, Brandon and Leah Monson, Lori Moerbitz, Matt Alarcon, Gloria Allan, Heather Kothbauer, Megan Hepokoski, Laura Pekuri, Sonya Young, Crystal Armstrong, and numerous other friends and clients all deserve sincere thanks for contributing inspiration which benefits the coaching practices used at Perception Coaching® LLC.

Capturing the spirit and practices of Perception Coaching® has been a journey full of detours, slowed progress, wonderful insight, and sustained effort. I am extremely grateful to my family for their support and contributions. Steve Bengtson long ago stopped asking how the book is going, I assume to provide space for the work. Instead, he continued to contribute effort and support so that I and Perception Coaching® LLC would survive the sustained focus on writing. Haley Bengtson deserves thanks as a successful facilitator and coach who contributes both expertise and effort to support clients and Perception Coaching® LLC. As my coach, she focuses my efforts to communicate more effectively; through our sessions I was inspired to limit the amount of "Barb-speak" that clutters this work and incorporate other elements such as bias boxes and coaching practices. Thank you, Rob Duncan, for encouraging Haley's coaching career! Thank you to Will and Majora Bengtson for being indispensable supporters of both Perception Coaching® LLC and our coaching practices. Fulfilling roles from building management to bookkeeping to facilitating workshops they continue to contribute their diverse talents to this family business.

Finally, thank you for taking the time to read this! I hope you are kind enough to suspend judgment as you read ideas that may not resonate, looking for the gold which you can use to inspire your own talent and coaching practices.

Perception
Coaching

PART 1

DOI: 10.4324/9781003332770-1

Evolution

Perception Coaching® is the result of an intense curiosity regarding shifting intentions from survival to success over decades of exploration, experience, and learning.

Converging paths

How can so many people perceive their own great potential, yet struggle to see their best path to success and strive for it? My quest to explore this question started in the 1970s. At that time success seemed exceptional; many people were doing things, yet very few people appeared to achieve success. While I was surrounded by friends and classmates with great potential, to my naïve mind most struggled to do well. Successes and failures appeared to be random. One individual would interrupt to respond to a question and be commended, another would be admonished for speaking out of turn. Many people seemed to be doing similar things, yet they had wildly different results. I could not understand or explain the factors at work and attributed much of the variation to luck. Throughout my life and careers, I have paid particular attention to evidence of talents around me and the diverse situations of the people who have them.

As a young learner I chased perfection, reveling in report cards with straight A's. Academically I was relatively successful, in that I could learn the way most teachers taught. Like that of many in early adolescence, I went to junior high school and my life seemed to fall apart. I did not see the relevance of study skills, so did not take any time or opportunities to develop them. I exerted little effort and was likely seen as an underachiever. This continued through high school.

Then, I went to college for computer engineering; I enjoy logic and math and was excited to focus on some *real* work which would lead to my career. I faced inconsistent performance in my first attempts at college. Some classes were easy, and I performed well; others felt more difficult, yet I still enjoyed sporadic success. I tried different courses, professors, and academic pursuits, searching for the key to the exceptional performances I had as a young learner. Frustrated that I could not find a strategy or clue for consistent success, I started working full time and taking classes part time, until I stopped taking courses altogether.

Marriage and children followed. I was determined to support the success of my children, wanting them to get more from their education than I managed to accomplish. I still believed that college had answers, so I returned to the university setting as a student of teacher education. Through my purpose, I found I was now able to perform consistently well. As I searched for ways to support learning, I found notable gaps in my own learning, and identified some of my learning talents. Experiences pursuing my undergraduate degree while raising children helped me see what I could not before; all talents come with needs, blind spots, and successes. When we overuse our talents, they show up as weaknesses and create barriers to success.

As a teacher, I often taught talented and gifted students in math and language arts. In this atmosphere I continued to work to untie the knot which is inconsistent results when extraordinary talents are present. My teaching style is that of supporting alongside learners, contrasted with the instructional style of traditional teaching in front of learners. In the classroom we focused our work on problem-solving skills, study skills, and conceptual development; I felt this expertise and approach were what the students needed to succeed. There were students who would do everything, including exploring and producing high-quality work, others who would just check the box meeting expectations and nothing more, and yet others who would not meet expectations. These differences appeared to be uncorrelated with academic ability; there had to be other identifiable factors at work. When we were doing math problem solving, one bright student told me that I was not teaching, that I should tell them what to do. There are many individuals who feel the teacher's role is to tell learners what to do and how to do it, favoring declarative and procedural knowledge. This was a clue I pursued by looking for ways to support the affective aspects of learning. My first focus in graduate school was on engagement and motivation. I balanced my discovery style with scaffolded guidance for those who sought it; this approach alleviated tensions for some, and more students appeared to enjoy coming to and participating in classes. However, challenges remained when it came to completing work, making responsible decisions, and other behaviors. During teacher conferences, when students had trouble handing in work or struggled with other academic behaviors, parents and students alike expressed the notion that *a smart person should be able to do this!* The implication being "smart" is global, applicable to all thinking as well as behaviors; if one is smart and "tries harder" they will succeed. We met challenges with strategies which increased engagement and caring more about investing in our learning; these efforts supported a few more learners, but all were not yet flourishing.

My next endeavor to effectively support learners came in pursuing a PhD. My goal included exploring how learning happens and is utilized, specifically focused on processes relevant to cognition, learning, and problem solving. Through this study I gained appreciation for the contributions and limited capacities of attention and working memory, and the impact of variability in individual capacities as an interaction with preferences.

Misconceptions are commonly addressed in the classroom, although not always effectively. Repeating, rewording, and showing accurate information are techniques that likely create cognitive dissonance but not a clear path for processing or re-thinking to change existing faulty knowledge. The implicit processes related to attention and storage which must occur before a learner has any hope at retrieval or application reveal many opportunities to miss information, alter or distort information to fit established beliefs, and otherwise introduce bias or misunderstanding. The path from sensing complex information to the ensuing cognitive interactions suggests attention to awareness and engagement are essential to improve clarity and access in learning environments. To impact the behavioral aspects of learning educators must provide clear, meaningful expectations; clarity is added to learning objectives with reflection on both what we ask of learners and how we support their efforts to meet expectations.

I worked on my dissertation evenings and was a classroom teacher during the day, simultaneously immersed in theory, practice, and effectively bridging the two. Thanks to a forward-thinking administrator, Susan Burris, a coaching program was developed in our school district. I was selected by my peers to be the coach in our school and shifted from classroom teacher to teacher on special assignment. This role added a new element to my mission to improve student outcomes. How might I support the efforts of my fellow teachers, teachers who work independently to meet the needs of their students in their classrooms, and are overburdened by committees, supervision times, continued professional development, standardized assessments, and curriculum changes, to name a few of their other responsibilities.

Because teacher education programs and licensing include standardized recommended practices and content, many teachers with excellent content knowledge and classroom management systems assume their peers have similar skills, values, and passions for education. However, all teachers experience unique classrooms as well as other learning opportunities as children; these greatly influence their learning while in teacher education and in turn their teaching practice. Finding value in differences was once again brought to the forefront of my work. Educational approaches vary greatly, and individual teacher preferences are reflected in their diverse classroom practices. In their classrooms, teachers shine, doing what they do best. As a coach I observed many excellent practices and techniques that if shared would improve learning outcomes for more students. Teachers take pride in their personal excellence and tend to safeguard it; this makes sharing and development both essential and sometimes difficult.

Each educator brings their own talents to the work of teaching. The diversity of teacher talents which students experience over their education may only sporadically align with their diverse learning needs. Through the coaching program, professional learning communities formed to give teachers a dedicated, weekly venue to share their talents, techniques, and workload, in an effort to more consistently and predictably support students with diverse experiences and learning styles. Together teachers work to understand each other, address standards, design and implement evaluation, and improve management. While supporting teachers and developing as a coach, I earned my PhD and continued in my role as teacher on special assignment for another three years. I was highly motivated by the challenging, impactful, and rewarding work of supporting educators. My next career phase started so that I could broaden the impact potential of coaching as a development tool.

Putting it together

Each phase in life provides opportunities to learn, fail, succeed, and grow. Through the process, themes related to interests, challenges, and approach become visible. For me, lifelong themes include a sustained deep interest in learning, recognition that all individuals possess talents, that different approaches can be effective to meet any one goal, and this byproduct of evaluating classroom experiences and teacher training: individuals can reach wildly different conclusions, even when presented with the same content in the same context while working together. I have learned that coaching, with its approach of individualized and sustained support, is the most effective development tool to support excellence as well as bridge knowledge gaps and knowing-doing gaps. Coaching improves well-being and productivity in workplaces and the community.

In 2016 I retired as a public school educator and immersed myself in research and development efforts dedicated to performance coaching.

Perception Coaching® was established to empower others, grounded in the idea that one can and should *set your sail* for success.

'Tis The Set Of The Sail (One Ship Sails East)
By Ella Wheeler Wilcox (1850–1919)

But to every mind there openeth,
A way, and way, and away,
A high soul climbs the highway,
And the low soul gropes the low,
And in between on the misty flats,
The rest drift to and fro.

But to every man there openeth,
A high way and a low,
And every mind decideth,
The way his soul shall go.

One ship sails East,
And another West,
By the self-same winds that blow,
'Tis the set of the sails
And not the gales,
That tells the way we go.

Like the winds of the sea
Are the waves of time,
As we journey along through life,
'Tis the set of the soul,
That determines the goal,
And not the calm or the strife.

This poem (Wilcox, 1913) captures the spirit Perception Coaching® applies to well-being, productivity, and innovation. When you are intentional in setting and pursuing your direction, your goals inform your decisions, provide hope for the future, and support continuous progress toward your objectives, even in the face of obstacles and distractions.

That is not to say life will be devoid of strife. Perception Coaching® works to reduce the apparent inconsistencies of thought and performance to help efforts become more effective and efficient. Our goal is to increase successes experienced by individuals and organizations, starting by recognizing preferences, including talents. Preferences provide insight to understand the power and limitations of what we sense so that we may navigate challenges, be productive, and find better ways forward while being our authentic selves.

For me, Perception Coaching® is a mission-driven endeavor. I welcome and appreciate your presence in the coaching world and hope the ideas herein support your efforts!

Introduction

We are each our own first coaching client. As you first read an idea, imagine how you can use it to coach yourself. As you dig deeper, reflect on your talents, perceptions, and the implications of the processes and strategies described. How might you coach yourself, or someone with your perspectives, to strive for well-being? How do your talents support your productivity? How do your perceptions shape your understanding of the world? Recognize how your perspective and preferences support you as you stretch to be more effective.

By first understanding ourselves, we develop clarity around how we sense talents and needs in others as well as the world around us. Many sections include bias boxes; the information therein adds transparency regarding preferences which influence aspects of the Perception Coaching® approach and provides an opportunity to consider and add your own preferences.

Then, begin to seek out and sense the diverse talents of others; notice talents that align with your preferences as well as those which complement your talents. Consider how others might respond to questions regarding well-being, productivity, and understanding the world. Be open to sensing talents and appreciating the talents of others. When talents are recognized, the needs and tensions experienced by others become clearer.

A caution as you try on some of the ideas, especially as you use them to support others: consider the preferences, needs, and talents you sense in others as *hypotheses*. Talk to them to verify or test that what you sense also makes sense to them. To avoid influencing their response with your perspective, ask open-ended questions about their talents and preferences with authentic curiosity. Facilitating dialogue about talents is a great means to connect with and begin to understand others.

Finally, to apply the content to coaching practices consider how will you extend your learning and use your talents to support others. How do your talents help you connect learning and action? How do you build trust? What strategies do you have for effective dialogue? How might you help others to identify, develop, and use their best strategies to succeed?

Effective Perception Coaching® relies on your positive intent, self-awareness, and curiosity. The ideas here provide perspectives and tools to support your work. Everyone starts with varying skills, talents, and experiences which make some aspects of Perception Coaching® intuitive, others joyful, and yet others challenging. You may want to jump to a specific topic or follow a more linear path through the book; let your needs and preferences lead the way.

Overview

Topics which translate well to becoming one's purpose include goal and effort statements. These are in part a reminder that any goal requires physical and/ or mental effort; see this as a beginning to consider what must be accomplished to support progress toward success. Part 1 provides insights to the Perception Coaching® model and interacting with others as a coach. Parts 2–3 explore three topics which address most performance needs. First is well-being, including sense of self and navigating life and social situations. Next is a focus on productivity, from goals and planning to meeting challenges. Last is innovation, which is solution oriented with attention to the topics of opportunity, creativity, and purpose. Innovation is a synthesis both leveraging and improving elements of well-being and productivity. The contents are organized to be accessible whether the book is navigated cover to cover or used as a strategic resource.

Set your sail and enjoy the journey!

Best regards,

Barb

Coaching approach
1

Goal: Facilitate others' efforts to gain clarity, consider alternatives, and develop their best strategies and solutions to succeed. Coaching interactions build others' confidence in their ability to grow, pursue goals, and be resilient in the face of challenge.

Efforts: Coaching interactions center on others' expertise about their own life and their ability to determine their best solutions. Coaches listen, question, and respond effectively to engage others' knowledge and sense of perspective.

Fred's worry

I was enjoying lunch with fellow coaches, sharing challenges, celebrating successes, and talking business, when we were interrupted by a friend who had a worry. Seeing the assorted expertise at the table, and knowing our appreciation for interesting situations, Fred shared that their eldest child is going to college next year and they are worried about the change. Fred was immediately met with two useful and very different responses.

One coaching companion asked if the child had committed to a college. *Not yet*, was the answer. That coach followed up by asking about progress on college applications and tours.

Another coach at the table asked how the family handles change. Fred mentioned that they had recently moved homes while remaining in the same school district. There ended up being many changes and it seemed to work out just fine. The follow-up question this coach asked was, *How may going to college be like the recent move?*

DOI: 10.4324/9781003332770-2

Fred thanked us for letting them interrupt our lunch and went off to meet their lunch companion. We continued the conversation; each coach providing context related to their approach to Fred's worry.

Coach one began by saying that being prepared to go to college is a process which is time dependent. College-related worries often stem from the uncertainty of change and the number of necessary tasks to make it happen, including all the preparation, selecting the right place, and eventually the moving process. They ended their explanation by noting that a coach familiar with college preparation supports clients by uncovering blind spots. They also support planning to make the process efficient and effective for the client.

Coach two noted that shifting a worry of the unknown to more familiar territory helps clients connect, adapt, and lean on skills they already possess. A coach who works with a client to relate existing tensions to familiar contexts and accomplishments supports well-being. They facilitate shifting client worries about unpredictable change to thinking about using their talents and abilities to effectively navigate change.

Both approaches are beneficial; one is focused on productivity and the process while the other focuses on well-being and transferring skills. The approach which aligns with Fred's preferences and needs is the best approach for Fred, and that could be one, both, or neither of these.

Reflect and discuss

As you peruse this section and interact with clients, consider answering and adapting the following:

1. What perspectives are potentially relevant to consider regarding Fred's worry?
2. Do either of the approaches shared by the two coaches resonate with you? How?
3. How might you leverage your expertise to respond to Fred?

The effort required to center your focus on the client's narrative as you listen and respond can be substantial when you naturally see a viable solution path. Consider your responses to the reflection questions and how you might best support facilitating client development. What is your approach? Clarifying your coaching approach starts with exploring your perspectives as an individual and coach. Then, with your perspectives in mind, seek to understand the Perception Coaching® skills and strategies and how you might leverage them. Finally, explore how your expertise and preferences interact with the diverse development roles you may be asked to fill; understand your capacity to meet expectations and draw limits. As you consider the following ideas, keep in mind how they each may influence your potential responses to Fred's worry.

Coach perspective

Everyone has preferences, the formation of which are influenced by many factors. What one has done, how time is spent, and what work is pursued are experiences that both influence and indicate preferences. If you had a career before coaching, the work, professional development, and performance expectations you experienced all contribute to your understanding of learning, goals, and success and will therefore impact your coaching perspective. Themes related to interests become visible when reflecting on experience. Over time, you build systems of expertise that align with your strongest interests and preferences.

Interests include things to which one is drawn, often the "go-to" when filling free time. An interest may be enjoyable, functional, or serve a larger purpose. For example, consider jigsaw puzzles. They are an interest which some people enjoy while others do not. For those interested, building puzzles may serve as a metaphor for their life or reflect a tendency for bringing order to chaos. Completing puzzles can be satisfying for these individuals solely as an enjoyable activity, because it represents a sense of order, or perhaps by completing a puzzle they discover a strategy which when transferred to a complex issue helps uncover traits which lead to opportunities or solutions.

Your perspective is influenced by the things which occupy your mind or body with unusually high focus. The things that capture your attention and are noticed, maybe even distract you, when you are occupied with something else will influence your perceptions of the larger world. Explore patterns in life to identify interests which may be visible in collections, research, and hobbies. Interests may also be seen in activities, places, or pursuits to which one is drawn. Whether your interests are goal driven, immersive, or otherwise occupy thoughts or behaviors, they can be a source of insight and inspiration when considered in an intentional, relevant way, as suggested by the puzzle metaphor.

Your expertise has the potential to be your greatest source of impact when coaching. Your areas of interest likely indicate the expertise you are developing. Ten years or more of researching, practicing, and being a keen observer of a facet of life or work develops expertise. A timeframe of ten years of immersion is commonly accepted to be a prerequisite of expertise because one must first learn technical skills then practice them extensively over time to incrementally perfect technique across several aspects of performance in the focus area. This incremental, time-consuming process of development is readily observed and has been studied for public performers such as players of chess and musical instruments (Ericsson, 2003).

Over years of intentional practice, one goes beyond the expected and begins to shape a subject or discipline. Many practice techniques to become technically perfect and perform consistently well, meeting the highest expectations of their craft. An expert does more; while performing in ways which are technically perfect, their performance is uniquely identifiably as their own in nuance, visible in how they create and respond to the unexpected.

Niche is often an idea suggested when coaching is pursued. It is a preference to explore, because having a niche is not necessary or required. Determining a niche may create focus for development, practice, and messaging; it also may provide unnecessary limits to development and opportunities. Exploring your perspective in the areas of expertise, preferences, or observed needs can lead to choosing a specialization, likely to become coaching expertise over time. Existing expertise to consider may be in the form of content, methods, or skills. Consider tasks you execute or knowledge you use flawlessly and with style on a regular basis or easily on demand – these may indicate a niche audience. Preferences may show up as strengths, those natural ways of doing, relating, or thinking that lead to optimal results. This may lead one to specialized processes or to shift practice to focus on working with teams, or leaders with specific areas of strengths in mind. Finally, if you notice an unfulfilled need or group of people who may benefit from specialized support, you may develop means to coach unique content to meet these needs – the needs experienced in specific roles or industries, for example. Niche can also be developed through practice, noticing trends in client success or affinity. Once again, having a niche is your prerogative and should be connected to your coaching perspective.

Reflect and discuss

1. What preferences and expertise do you have that support your efforts?
2. How does your expertise support the development of others?

Your skills in action:

3. What aspect of Fred's worry interests you, aligns with your experiences or expertise, or brings to your mind a question? Explain.

Development

The work of coaching explores and develops perceptions, attitudes, and approaches; these are the underlying systems which influence how and what we think. Coaches work to support people to clarify purpose and explore barriers; coaches help with the ongoing experiments people do to thrive, be productive, and seize opportunities. Space for clients to develop strategies, efficiently and effectively set goals, and define measures of success is held in coaching sessions. Coaching processes and solutions are different than those of clinical settings. Therapists, counselors, and other licensed profession-als delve into the past to heal wounds, fix wrongs, address dysfunction, or create closure; these needs and processes are never a part of coaching ses-sions. Coaching clients are generally well and striving to improve their cur-rent attitude, performance, or potential so they may seize current and future opportunities.

Conversations with an individual about their experiences, what they have tried, and how they succeed are instrumental to coaching. Clients explore their best strategies to leverage their efforts and ways of doing, thinking, and relating; the coach provides focus, space, perspective, and expertise which support clients' efforts to pursue their goals. Coaches do not see clients for crises of any type, emotional, physical, or mental. Coaching is not appropri-ate for clients in crisis; they must be referred to professionals trained for such work. Refer a client for support when they respond in a manner or bring up a subject which raises concerns for their safety or may indicate a risk to oth-ers. Err on the side of caution; stop the conversation and suggest a clinical psychologist, therapist, or counselor to support your client's immediate focus and needs. The client's return to coaching occurs when they are no longer on the brink of, or in, crisis.

To avoid possible conflicts, clearly define the potential as well as the limi-tations your skills contribute to your coaching practice and persona. This is especially important when your experience and expertise include educa-tion, training, counseling, therapy, or other licensed or certified professions. What is coaching and what is not a part of your coaching must be clear in your mind so the intentions of your interactions, responses, and role remain clear.

Coaching is personalized, future-oriented development. Probabilities are less relevant than possibilities when considering data and multiple strategies. Performance coaches build relationships with clients, working to understand their unique talents, preferences, and experiences to support their efforts to strive for their best results.

The focus on development can take many forms, including coaching, training, and teaching.

Bias box

Delivering development

Coaching with individual differences in mind is more effective than using development approaches which focus on content and strategies shown to be statistically significant or work for most people.

Exploring factors, traits, and statistically significant findings in the field of development leads one to question and hypothesize the application of such findings. When quality information about performance is scientifically derived and objectively summarized, it is of value to coaching. Data and statistics which describe factors, how they are related, how frequently they occur, and how these factors influence or interact with performance are especially meaningful to development. However, statistically significant data are not facts which apply to everyone; every individual is likely to have at least one unlikely characteristic and it cannot be assumed that likely factors accurately describe a specific individual.

Coaching: Coaching is a flexible development approach designed to build relationships for the purpose of effectively responding to specific client needs. Individuals have unique experiences, goals, ways of doing things, and gifts and challenges; the best strategy for one individual may not be useful for another.

Selecting strategies to share or explore is achieved through conversation; client experiences and preferences determine the tools clients will find useful to succeed. Coaches who are working in areas of expertise introduce adapted strategies, rather than those used by most people.

Training: Training is an efficient development approach designed to deliver role or position-relevant content set by the trainer or organization. Training occurs as part of a system to improve performance by developing skills or sets of skills with consistent delivery of primarily declarative and procedural knowledge.

Coaches use training approaches in group presentations as an efficient means to introduce themselves and share their processes, services, or tools with potential clients. Consistency is key in these types of appearances to increase visibility and encourage trust and brand recognition.

Teaching: Teaching is an adaptable approach to conceptual development which uses best practices to share a wide variety of important ideas and strategies to support the general growth of learners. Teaching addresses diverse learning strategies and content is delivered with a scope and sequence in mind, much like training.

Coaches use teaching to introduce clients and potential clients to their areas of expertise. The goal is to select and share ideas useful to the audience; some participants will benefit from further exploration through coaching.

Explore your preferences for development. For each pair mark the strength of your preference between the two anchors; the center is neutral, indicating no preference.

Coaching ---- 3 ---- 2 ---- 1 ---- 0 ---- 1 ---- 2 ---- 3 ---- **Teaching**
Coaching ---- 3 ---- 2 ---- 1 ---- 0 ---- 1 ---- 2 ---- 3 ---- **Training**
Training ---- 3 ---- 2 ---- 1 ---- 0 ---- 1 ---- 2 ---- 3 ---- **Teaching**

Note the order and strength of your preferences.

Reflect and discuss

Consider the purpose, values, and benefits of the three development approaches:

1. Describe circumstance or content for which development is best accomplished by:

   - adapting for individual differences
   - efficient and consistent skill acquisition
   - identifying the best strategies for most.

2. Considering how content is delivered, do you prefer to train, teach, or coach? Why?
3. How does this align with sharing your expertise to contribute to your coaching perspective?

Tenets

Coaching is a connected development process focused on next-level success, somewhat like teaching. As a classroom educator, one rule I implemented when working with students was that their writing instrument should remain in their hands when doing their work. When a teacher takes a pencil to "show" a student how to do something, they take more than the pencil from the student, they change the dynamic of the student's approach to their work, impacting their confidence and important points of reference. Another rule I have concerns *wait time*; following a question or prompt, provide extra quiet or thinking time to allow more learners to respond rather than rewarding and building from the first answer. This encourages deep thinking, alternative views, and time for everyone to develop ideas and join the discussion. As an added benefit, we learn together that good questions generate a variety of good responses. These strategic rules guided my teaching, improving my ability to support learners while respecting their differences. Similarly, creating and adhering to coaching tenets benefits both the coach and client.

It is important to remember that clients enter the coaching relationship to support their efforts and goals. Joseph and Bryant-Jefferies (2019) discuss how coaching is a person-centered approach, an adaptation of Carl Rogers' evolution of his 1940s non-directive therapy. Rogers posited that people naturally seek growth; occasional outside support when they face incongruencies helps them progress. Coaches who appreciate that individuals naturally direct their development over their lifetime also recognize their support of these efforts occurs for a relatively short time and with limited context, as shared by the client. To ensure coaching is supportive and not overtly leading I remind myself of these tenets:

1. The client is the expert regarding their life and perspectives.
2. The client chooses and pursues their best paths.
3. The client's efforts and knowledge produce their best results.
4. The coach supports progress on goals.
5. The coach provides support and space to live authentically.
6. The coach responds authentically and without judgment.

These tenets are reflected in both the approaches and practices of Perception Coaching®. Whenever you meet, whether for a quick call, in-person discussion, via email correspondence, or combinations of these and other modes, keep your intention true. Consider the relevance of these beliefs as you explore strategies, questions, and perspectives.

Reflect and discuss

1. Do these tenets resonate? How might you adapt them or put them in your own words?
2. What possible ways can your expertise and perspective interfere with your focus on your clients' perspectives?
3. What tenets may you add to guide your coaching?
4. Compile a list of tenets to be a living document, one which you revise as you develop your coaching practice.
    a. What is a convenient format or media for such a list?
    b. How can it also serve to keep guidelines, questions, and strategies easily accessible as your coaching practice develops?

In summary, when coaching, listen as the client's stories direct your attention to your related expertise and interest areas. While their well-being, needs, and goals remain the focus of coaching conversations, your coaching perspective always joins and influences the discussion. Because of this, you must be acutely aware of your expertise and share with clear purpose, keeping the client at the center of the discussion. When a client's need is especially intense and immediate, or you become uncomfortable with their talk or behaviors, refer them to an appropriate professional.

Additionally, coaching sessions provide space to encourage, challenge, and celebrate your client's efforts with their goals in mind. As a coach, your approaches to meeting these expectations are uniquely yours, informed by coaching perspectives. If communication is clear and adherence to tenets is not meeting the needs of a client, the coach–client relationship is likely not a good fit. The goal is then to seek a best fit dynamic, when the coach's approach, skills, and manner are beneficial to the client's skills, needs, and learning modes.

Coach and client skills

The depth of your knowledge and experience is key to responding authentically and productively to client situations, emotions, needs, and successes. Intense focus on the client's story builds understanding and facilitates connecting relevant aspects of the client's experiences to your expertise. Attention to listening, prompting, and responses improves conversations and more effectively supports clients in a manner which values their well-being and objectives. Because the coaching relationship is an alliance, clients need to be willing to enter the coaching dynamic, communicate authentically, and commit to efforts that contribute to their success.

Bias box

Client willingness

If a client is willing to navigate communication preferences and needs with the coach, other factors for client willingness can be achieved.

Client willingness is a precursor to coaching success. Buy-in is essential for a client to benefit from coaching. People may come to coaching out of curiosity; there is likely a hope or need associated with this which can be explored to determine if coaching is a good fit. Some individuals have a goal and come to a coach to explore means to achieve it, while others seek accountability to support progress on their plan. Clients may be sponsored by an employer who connects them with coaching to reach their high potential or as support for a professional improvement plan. Whatever the purpose of coaching, clients must be willing to develop an alliance with the coach, communicate authentically, and expend effort.

Collaborators: In coaching relationships a mutual agreement is developed through clear expectations regarding how the coach will operate and the responsibilities of the client. Together coach and client address confidentiality and types of support to determine both the scope of coaching and related limitations.

This aspect has the potential to determine if coach and client are a good fit with the added benefit of establishing the direction or goal of coaching sessions. This is an essential step particularly when the coach's or client's primary concern is return on investment or accountability.

Communication: Communication in coaching must be authentic, clear, and meaningful. Developing effective communication between coach and client requires navigation, each reaching out to understand the other and develop common language for relevant ideas.

Coach and client must find the right balance between alignment and differences. Aligned communication creates an efficient, supportive environment. Differences make mutual understanding difficult, though working through them creates great potential for seeing beyond one's own perspective.

Effort: Development and progress require cognitive and behavioral effort. When related to coaching, effort is directed at the goal or a portion of it, effects are processed, and next action steps are set and carried out.

Finding the right actions, strategies, and paths to follow is often the primary purpose of coaching. Clients willing to experiment, fail, and continue working will reap the benefits of their efforts.

Self-assess

Which factors of client willingness are most relevant to you? For each pair mark the strength of your preference between the two anchors; the center is neutral, indicating no preference.

Collaborators ---- 3 ---- 2 ---- 1 ---- 0 ---- 1 ---- 2 ---- 3 ---- **Communication**
Collaborators ---- 3 ---- 2 ---- 1 ---- 0 ---- 1 ---- 2 ---- 3 ---- **Effort**
Effort ---- 3 ---- 2 ---- 1 ---- 0 ---- 1 ---- 2 ---- 3 ---- **Communication**

Note the order and strength of your preferences.

Reflect and discuss

Consider the purpose, values, and benefits of the three client willingness perspectives:

1. Describe circumstance or content for which client connection is best accomplished by:
    - coach and client alliance
    - developing common language
    - capacity to expend effort.
2. Considering the relevance of client willingness, do you prefer to start with assurance regarding alliance, communication, or effort? Why?
3. How might you explore these aspect(s) to support willingness for a client who enjoys learning and is resistant to change?
4. How does this contribute to your coaching perspective?

Coaching conversations

Coaching relationships are grounded in the understanding that clients are the experts in their lives and work. Coaches strive to support the efforts of clients to find their next best action using the clients' own experiences and expertise. Given this, arguably the most valuable aspect of a coaching session is a powerful question with potential to prompt a memory or new connection to their expertise, one which adds perspective or a path to progress on their goal. The interactions of listening, questioning, and responding, though presented in that order below, are not always used as a linear process. Strategic selection and application of these skills is borne out of keen awareness and attention to the flow of client information and their preferences for feedback.

Listen for talents, needs, and themes: A coach's most powerful tool is holistic listening. Listen with reference to the context of previous conversations and listen presently to the whole person, including verbal and nonverbal communication. A perceptive coach will focus their attention to detect themes, missed perspectives, hidden solutions, and attitudes. With listening as your primary focus, consider the purpose of every response you share including nonverbals like nods, smiles, and questioning glances. Strategically embed opportunities to check your understanding with paraphrasing or summarizing; these interactions should be limited and demonstrate engagement and encourage elaboration. The client's thinking progression sets the main conversational path; any detour you add with questions, or your thoughts, should be purposeful and short, quickly looping back to the main, client-centered path.

Pose powerful questions and prompts for more information: What themes, needs, or possibilities do you hear? Which ideas when explored will contribute to the client's purpose? When you contemplate an appropriate way to respond, question, or next steps, take a breath and take time to think deeply about what your client is sharing. Is their purpose clear? Do you have authentic questions about details or impact? Do you have an insight you would like them to consider? Questions you pose during client processing or stories are beneficial when intention is clear, whether it be to challenge thinking, prompt reflection, or provide clarity. Each question should stand alone and include sufficient wait time. Work to recognize and be responsive to your client's conversational style, and question with their preferences in mind.

Some people are puzzlers and when they think of a great question, they automatically think of possible answers. They then pose the question in terms of these answers; designed to eliminate the obvious, or to provide choice or a starting point for the reply. If this describes you, resist the urge; this leads and limits responses! Start with the most open, least defined question related to the focus topic to get authentic, informative replies. People share better information through dialogue; the mutual process of seeking to clarify a vague, open-ended question provides insights, too.

Respond with observations and expertise: The strategies, content knowledge, and experience you bring are important. Clients will reach a point in their story or explanation when they expect a coaching response. Consider insights you gleaned from the client's story; purposefully select what you might pursue, share, or question, and what is best kept to yourself or saved for another time.

You will find times when it is appropriate to share stories with related content. Your experience and expertise are coaching superpowers; no one else has your unique perspective. Tell relevant stories about your experiences or create anecdotal learning opportunities which demonstrate strategy use, illustrate decision-making skills, or add context to alternative perspectives. An effective and relatable narrative will engage and build rapport with your client. If you share too much your story becomes the focus, and the client is secondary; work to keep the client as the primary storyteller.

Bias box

Coaching skills

Listening is the most powerful tool for coaches because client stories provide essential insights from which to craft powerful questions and supportive responses.

The most important coaching skills are those which create a client-centered dialog. In an hour session, the first half is often spent understanding the client's experience since the last session. If it is the first session, that first half is spent listening for goals, what has been tried, and experiences around the goal. Then clients explore what is working, what is challenging, and their hopes for the future. The final quarter or so is dedicated to identifying an action for commitment, and may include suggestions, strategies, or other input from the coach.

Listen: Client stories provide the context and perspective needed to provide effective and efficient support that meets their unique needs. Holistic listening requires high engagement, with attention focused on words, tone, body language, and energy. Good listening benefits from experience to recognize themes or changes in the characteristic expressions used by the client.

Narratives describe the client's recognized reality, provide important context to complement goals, and pose opportunities to explore perceptions and assumptions. Close listening is required to notice the client's bold statements, actions taken, emotions experienced, and how they are thinking about their story.

Prompt: Exercise curiosity. Tell me more, authentic questions, as well as nods or silence encourage clients to add valuable details and insights to their stories. One client may share a stream of consciousness without any need for prompts while another shares readily without prompts, though requires quiet space as they process before speaking.

The art of prompts is in aligning them with what works best for the client. Individual preferences can be discussed explicitly or understood experientially, through observation of effects of different prompting strategies.

Respond: Responding influences clients' perspectives and processing, so is best done after clients share and process their experiences. A response provides an opportunity for clients to reflect on their experience, have insights, and reach conclusions. Coaches support these efforts with appropriate responses.

Use your expertise. Suggest strategies with *Have you tried…* add perspective with *How might someone else see this?* or share themes detected in their story to add opportunities for insights.

Self-assess

Explore your talents and preferences for contributing to coaching conversations. For each pair mark the strength of your preference between the two anchors; the center is neutral, indicating no preference.

Listen ---- 3 ---- 2 ---- 1 ---- 0 ---- 1 ---- 2 ---- 3 ---- **Prompt**
Listen ---- 3 ---- 2 ---- 1 ---- 0 ---- 1 ---- 2 ---- 3 ---- **Respond**
Respond ---- 3 ---- 2 ---- 1 ---- 0 ---- 1 ---- 2 ---- 3 ---- **Prompt**

Note the order and strength of your preferences.

Reflect and discuss

Consider the purpose, values, and benefits of these three aspects of conversation:

1.   Describe talents and strategies you have related to each coaching skill:
     - Listening focused on client's story
     - Prompts for elaboration which don't shift focus from client
     - Responding without directing

2.   Clients and coaches glean insights from coaching conversations.

     - What conversational strategies do you use which provide clients with time and resources to create insightful "ah-ha" moments?
     - How and when do you share your insights?

3.   How does this set of preferences contribute to your coaching perspective?

Mission in mind

Coaching meetings are clients' dedicated appointments with their goal work, necessary because day-to-day life is full to overflowing for individuals and organizations. Coaching makes space and sustains focused attention on successful attainment of goals while busy, high-achieving, and overburdened clients work to enjoy and take care of their complex lives. Coaching clients are generally motivated to achieve an outcome or goal.

The power of coaching sessions includes the impact meetings have on choices. Coaches facilitate progress in part by identifying decision points during coaching conversations. Identifying and selecting focal topics and strategies is significant work in itself; spend time ensuring good fit objectives within the discussion and planning for between-session work. When a commitment is set for what will be done before the next meeting, it creates a nudge for the client before or sometimes at the beginning of the next meeting, depending on individual preferences and factors. A nudge may be an overt reminder for the client, or it may be an internal pressure to act, to avoid disappointment or wasting time talking about "why something was not done" during a coaching conversation. Van Gestel et al. (2021) found nudges to be an effective means to support individuals to act as they intended. Coaching provides space, perspective, and strategies *just in time*, while providing the support and nudges a client needs to focus their efforts and continue to create progress.

Reflect and discuss

Client willingness and coaching ability converge in coaching sessions. Purposeful planning will ensure quality interactions and conversations.

1. What aspects of your coaching perspective supports authentic questioning?
2. What skills do you have that may interfere with client thinking? How might you keep these in check?
3. What is the purpose of posing open questions to clients?
4. What influences how and when you use nudges?
5. How do your tenets support the ideas in this section? Will you revise, add, or remove any?
6. Capture quality questions. Compile a list of questions, perhaps where you keep your tenets, to revise as you develop your coaching practice.

Tools and strategies

Throughout this book diverse tools are referenced in context; powerful questions and other strategies have already been introduced. The following list is intended to *front load* a few more key ideas so that you can relate relevant strategies and tools as you navigate this resource and client interactions. This list includes transferable ideas with a direct link to the theoretical underpinnings of perception; it is not exhaustive. Ideas herein may be referenced later, embedded in more complex tools and strategies targeting specific topics.

Powerful questions for powerful processing and client stories

Questions are flexible tools essential to guiding client processing and meaningful coaching interactions. When simultaneously focused and open-ended, questions have power to elicit meaningful, authentic client stories. Given space and time to think in a journal or coaching session, reflection and seeking questions clarify connections, uncover preferences, provide evidence to understand implicitly sensed ideas, and otherwise support cognitive functions and learning which can be applied to development.

For example, pose questions like the following to explore talents, accomplishments, and goals to learn about client capacity and their ways of doing:

- What is your favorite part of your workday?
- What talents do you use every day?
- What is your greatest talent?
- What do you want to do more often?
- What do you want to do less often?
- What are your greatest accomplishments?
- What's a compliment you have received?

Reflection questions probe lived experience and are an effective tool to explore sense of self. The above reflection questions intentionally focus on affinity and success for the purpose of appreciation and identifying replicable means for achieving goals.

Seeking questions are powerful questions which support discovering new perspectives. Questions like the following are especially useful when clients explore the impact of their preferences or seek to increase perspective and trust in social situations:

- What follow-up question might you ask someone who seems to think like you?
- If a friend said that, what might you wonder?
- What talents might other people think you have?
- How might someone else see your decision?
- Does everyone feel that way about it?

Powerful questions elicit powerful stories. Some people are fluent storytellers and other require prompting to elaborate or clarify. If you sense there is more to a story or response, be ready with a prompt of "tell me more" or ask a relevant *how* or *why* question to support their efforts to elaborate on their story. Keep purpose and authenticity front of mind as you ask questions, improve on those you try, and generate new questions to support your clients' efforts.

Between-session work

When introducing a new idea or when awareness of or engagement with a topic seem in need of exploration or development, between-session work keeps the client actively engaged. This may include regular self-checks focused on the questions, *How am I with this topic?* Or *What real-life examples do I notice?*

Clients process according to preferences: this may be through reflective thinking, journaling, short messages, or otherwise collecting observations of the topic in everyday circumstances or through research. The qualitative data and accompanying feelings or conclusions are debriefed in the next coaching session by asking *what was... noticed, difficult, easy, or leads to next steps?*

Interrupt automaticity

Occasionally a client will come to coaching because they want to stop doing something. They may feel they talk too much, metaphorically stepping on others who are present. Perhaps they note that they judge others too quickly, respond harshly, or cannot say *no* and overcommit. Whatever it is, they perform the response automatically, without intention or consideration.

When an impulse is present, a pause provides time for the *automatic response* to dissipate. This is easy to say, and difficult to do because automaticity provides little time before the response begins. Understand the circumstances which trigger the automatic response, and prepare for and *engage interruption* using strategies like these:

1. When trigger circumstances are present, physically move, take a deep breath, mentally count to ten, or otherwise **act to interrupt** the automatic response and allow it to **dissipate**.
2. Consider a more appropriate response to replace the automatic response; **rehearse** using the productive response mentally or physically as appropriate. **Replace** the automatic response with the new, more productive response when circumstances are present.

Prioritize focus on *identifying and noticing cues*; interruption requires **awareness** to recognize when the automatic behavior is happening through noticing social cues, physical discomfort, or other **indicators** that the trigger circumstances are present. At first, the automatic response may start before the strategy to dissipate or replace can be implemented, which is why interruption requires both grace and tenacity. One may need to back down, stop and apologize, or mentally recalibrate to interrupt the behavior, then implement the plan for dissipation or replacement.

Developing and practicing new reactions takes time; especially sticky habits may require a referral to another professional. Strategies for **dissipation or replacement** of practiced thoughts and behaviors often require trial and error testing to find the most effective means to revise automatic responses. Through experimentation, needs, alternatives, and misunderstanding may be discovered. Changing automatic responses, when used as a strategy to address a performance concern, may uncover more serious needs. Coaches must always be aware of clients' needs and the scope of their practice; refer clients to a certified healthcare professional when circumstances indicate possible needs which are beyond the scope of coaching.

Suspend judgment

One will no longer be curious, explore, or learn if "the most relevant thing" about the people and things they observe is known. Labels, categories, and judgments are understanding endpoints; they provide closure to processing. *Suspend judgment* to short-circuit the part of implicit processing which labels observations. To do this one must insert doubt when conclusions seem to be reached; assume less to be more open to learning. This is especially true regarding people; the complexity of an individual's experiences, preferences, and life defies accurate, meaningful, or relevant labels. Suspending judgment is also effective for developing expertise or new perspectives when encountering related ideas, places, and other "known" things; it encourages seeking deeper understanding and allows for unique interpretations, connections, and applications.

Handling complexity

Tension may arise when one tries to understand or explain complex systems or issues. Ask clients how they deal with complex information. They may enjoy receiving a lot of information and organizing it with their preferences in mind, or they may prefer it to be delivered with support or systems in place. Tools and strategies to support complex ideas include analogy, outlines, lists, mapping categories, diagramming connections, or organizing using other visual models. Understanding how individuals organize their thinking in the presence of complexity is useful to support their efforts to meet their performance goals.

Card sorts

Jump past word generation and start with the higher order thinking skills of comparison and evaluation. Card sorts utilize pre-made word or picture decks. You may brainstorm these personally and create your own, or there are several concepts available, from favorite foods to core values. Instructions:

Look at each card and determine its relevance, then sort it to one of three piles. Adjust your three categories to make sense for the topic at hand such as:

- *Always* me / on my mind
- *Sometimes* me / may be a concern
- *Never* me / not relevant

Clients doing card sorts see several ideas in quick succession, dismissing those that are irrelevant and investing cognitive power on determining the value of those to which they are drawn. This process brings to the surface their preferences in the area addressed by the cards and may demonstrate how they process information. Do they spread out the cards and create hierarchies to relate ideas, naturally prioritize along the way, or do they follow your directions to sort by always, maybe, and never? Do they feel their perspective is missing from the cards? Observations of processing should be shared and discussed, perhaps by saying, "I noticed you grouped these things while sorting. Can you tell me about how they are related?"

The coaching debrief may take many forms depending on the goal and how they felt about the sorting process. If there are a great number of cards in the always pile, encourage removal of some. Strategies for this are to group similar and pick the best representation for the group or determine relevance of a card which can be seen as a parent card for those in the group. Alternatively, many cards selected as *always* can indicate that the topic is unclear or irrelevant, they have conflicting priorities, or lack core priorities. Discussion focuses on processing the client's questions, observations, and needs, though it may lean on the coach's experience with the activity for perspective. One may feel compelled to affirm choices, make reinforcing comments, or otherwise praise the effort of the activity. Avoid unnecessary feedback on client processing; much like in coaching conversations, feedback is authentic and intentional.

Assessments

Personality tests and other measures focusing on traits and characteristics are numerous. When used effectively, these provide valuable context and language to explore sense of self, as well as informing development preferences. Clients may come to you with DiSC®, Myers-Briggs' MBTI®, Gallup's CliftonStrengths®, and numerous other psychometric results, perhaps multiple assessments taken for different purposes. It is beneficial to spend time reviewing the information and ideas they provide concerning client preferences, talents, and needs. You can learn which types of information resonate and are valued by your client. Using the terms and language of your client's preferred assessment tool leverages its effectiveness by encouraging clarity and fluency specific to the characteristics measured. The use of common language from a valid assessment mitigates much of the confusion and misunderstanding introduced when individuals' characteristics are discussed using popular, ill-defined terms, like empathy or confidence, without the beneficial context an assessment tool provides.

Psychometric measures provide a systematic process for obtaining information about a particular phenomenon or factor regarding the participant's personality, talents, beliefs, values, attitudes, abilities, skills, interests, or characteristics. These should be administered and debriefed by a qualified individual. Bourne and Whybrow provide an excellent list of elements for effective feedback including specifics relating to listening, questioning, making connections, and feedback (2019, pp. 520–521).

Assessments gather data through interviews, observation, standardized tests, self-report measures, or other psychological measures. Common considerations associated with assessments include *reliability*, the degree to which it is trustworthy, free from random error, and produces the same results across multiple applications to the same sample, *validity*, that results are true, accurate, or based on established laws or theories, and *purpose*, how the results may be used; the level and type of risk associated with the use of the results should be aligned with the instruments' validity and reliability. Note, an assessment designed to determine job fit or which is used with other significant implications will indicate that purpose; using assessments for purposes outside of their intended use is malpractice.

Become well-versed in any assessment you use. As a Gallup® Certified Strengths Coach and EQ360/EQ-i²·⁰ Certified, the author's preference is to use these instruments in client development. The 34 talent themes of CliftonStrengths® support conversations which identify and guide the use of preferences and talents; results present the 34 in rank order and focus is on the dominant themes. Emotional intelligence skills and strategies are evaluated using EQ-i²·⁰ which is a norm-referenced assessment with 15 subscales; it may be used to determine role fit, unlike CliftonStrengths®. The EQ-i²·⁰ assessment is also valid to measure progress when it is given at the start and end of a coaching engagement because the effects of efforts directed to improve a specific set of subscales can be quantified by changes in scale scores; the author suggests a minimum of six months of coaching to produce noticeable change. You may be familiar with other measures and have other preferences. Be clear on the purpose and design of assessments to best support clients to use assessment results effectively and appropriately to make progress on their goals.

Reflection as a focused tool

Reflection provides insight for where attention focused and lingered and what may have been missed or misinterpreted. The goal is to broaden the definition of what is relevant, to revisit the experience with refocused attention, and become aware of additional information.

Self-reflection is an essential internal processing strategy, key to any phase of development. Self-reflection increases one's awareness of the significance of experiences; it uncovers how preferences show up and how attitudes interact with experience. Learning through reflection requires the client to be curious about the implications of their experiences, preferences, and attitudes; they then apply that learning to meet their current needs.

Below are *question stems* with suggested topics for reflection (select one to form a question):

- What is your self-talk when it comes to… (challenge, frustration, ease, failure, success)?
- How do you feel about feedback when it comes to… (giving, receiving, positive, negative, constructive) feedback?
- How do you feel about your… (abilities, preferences, opportunities, challenges, choices, experience)?

To extend beyond self-reflection, ask clients to explore alternative interpretations of their experiences, preferences, or attitudes, with the goal to broaden perceptions to support their development efforts. Consider providing *seeking questions* described in the "Powerful questions" section.

Check in with a scale report

Kilpatrick and Cantril discuss the utility of creating a self-anchoring scale in which a respondent defines the top (best) and bottom (worst) anchoring points in terms of their own relevant perceptions, goals, and values (1960). This self-defined scale is useful to detect perceived changes as support and / or development occurs. A simplified assessment, Cantril's Striving Scale (Ladder) can be used to collect quantitative data regarding well-being in the form of a step score; in his work, Cantril set step 10 at best possible life, step 0 at worst possible life (Tomyn, 2017). This methodology is also used for Gallup® Net Thriving in their global research (Clifton & Harter, 2021).

For convenience you may first use a ladder scale with Cantril's language as labels to explore client perceptions of the extremes and developmental steps in coaching conversations.

How are you?

10 = BEST POSSIBLE   **0** = WORST POSSIBLE

Figure 1.1 *How are you?* ladder scale sample. Illustration by the author.

Provide your client with a mental or real picture of a ladder with ten steps before eliciting a numeric response by asking: "If 10 is the best possible and 0 (the ground) is worst possible, what step are you on?" Wait time is recommended before further prompts or elaboration to provide sufficient time for the client to process and decide. This holistic score provides a great starting point for a discussion focused on how they came to select the number and how they perceive well-being.

Alternatively, the scale may be introduced to clients through discussion. Ask them for a phrase or example to describe "best," then a phrase or example for the "worst." Then share the ladder metaphor with their labels for 10 and 0. Clients may benefit from exploring labels for specific scale scores or steps: "At 10 am your reported score is step 6; what does that mean?" For best results, the ladder scale is a measure that is repeated and revisited. Regular use creates more consistent application and increases awareness of the measured concept.

Depending on client preferences, schedule, and needs they may want to check in with their state of being daily or multiple times per day.

As between-session work, clients may consider general well-being or a focus area for self-checks and record the scale measure at different times, a few times a day. This quantitative data is debriefed in the next coaching session by looking for patterns, reasons for extremes or lack of extremes, and results of actions taken to impact the measured factor.

Triad preference intensity scales

This tool explores the strength of a set of preferences in an important area. Bias boxes use this approach to consider relative preferences between three aspects, steps, or alternatives connected by the given concept. Often we think of preferences as a choice between two options; by adding a third factor, thinking expands beyond evaluating a given area as a dichotomy of this and not that by considering multiple related pairs and summarizing the findings.

The following example scale set explores needs. For each pair mark the strength of your preference between the two anchors; the center is neutral, indicating no preference.

Safety ---- O ---- O ---- O ---- O ---- O ---- O ---- O ---- Comfort
Safety ---- O ---- O ---- O ---- O ---- O ---- O ---- O ---- Purpose
Comfort ---- O ---- O ---- O ---- O ---- O ---- O ---- O ---- Purpose

Example results interpretation: For the following responses, *Comfort* appears to be a strong primary need bias and *Safety* is secondary; this respondent rarely prefers to pursue *purpose*.

Safety ---- O ---- O ---- O ---- O ---- O ---- X ---- O ---- Comfort
Safety ---- O ---- X ---- O ---- O ---- O ---- O ---- O ---- Purpose
Comfort ---- X ---- O ---- O ---- O ---- O ---- O ---- O ---- Purpose

For those who prefer quantifiable results, the scale may be numbered and summarized or interpreted as *Comfort = 5* and *Safety = 2*. Purpose was not a preference among these options.

Safety ---- 3 ---- 2 ---- 1 ---- 0 ---- 1 ---- X ---- 3 ---- Comfort (scored as Comfort = 2)
Safety ---- 3 ---- X ---- 1 ---- 0 ---- 1 ---- 2 ---- 3 ---- Purpose (scored as Safety = 2)
Comfort ---- X ---- 2 ---- 1 ---- 0 ---- 1 ---- 2 ---- 3 ---- Purpose (scored as Comfort = 3)

Users likely prefer either visual or numerical methods, finding one easier to understand; either representation provides results useful for the debrief and increasing understanding. Respondents who consider the meaning they discover when exploring their triad profile can apply increased understanding of preferences to their sense of self, ways of doing, or how they think about the area described by the three factors. Try using this tool in the bias boxes found throughout this book. Create your own scales with triads or groups of factors with your niche or expertise in mind. Consider common questions or observations that support understanding or navigating the world as content from which to glean preference sets of three elements, or more.

Reflect and discuss

Coaching skills and strategies:

1. How might you introduce one of the above strategies to a client while practicing the skills of listening, questioning, and responding?
2. How can the strategies outlined in this section empower a client?
3. What strategy or skill might you add to the above techniques?
4. How might communication skills support the structure for a client session?

    a. What other skills or purpose(s) would you add?
    b. Do these skills align with your coaching tenets?

Your skills in action:

5. When you consider Fred's worry, what comes to mind? Do you immediately have a solution? Do you have a question? Do you have several questions? When you consider Fred's worry, what strategies might you consider sharing with Fred?

Fluent and flexible skills

Clients with goals to increase confidence, start a career, or get more done find valuable perspective when a qualified coach supports exploration with their perceptions in mind. Coaches make preferences visible by using powerful questions that support purposeful reflection and stories detailing the successes they have experienced. A coach helps capture and connect the sources of clients' successes so that they may intentionally use them to create more success.

Well-being, productivity, and innovation capture the most frequent areas in which clients struggle or strive to improve. The ways in which coaches support clients in these areas are numerous and dynamic, dependent on types of clients and their purposes. Several factors increase success when coaching individuals, partners, teams, and scaling to organizations.

Coaching provides a powerful support system for an individual's development. Performance coaching starts with exploration for a clear sense of self and preferences; this is used to customize support so that clients can more effectively improve their well-being and optimize their ability to effectively navigate in and interact with the world. Individual clients often enter coaching to identify opportunities, develop professionally and personally, and improve performance with their well-being in mind. Perception Coaching® often includes questioning perceptions and judgments and developing strategies to increase energy, hope, and optimism. Learning- and cognition-informed strategies create useful touchpoints to explore and understand clients' current state and support client growth. Through discussion, clients become aware of their preferences and perceptions, evaluate the impact their current attitudes and understanding have on their perspective, and empower engagement with their naturally evolved processes to broaden perceptions and make progress toward goals. This does not happen in a vacuum.

With few exceptions, individuals are members of partnerships, teams, organizations, and communities. Individual development also addresses improving social interactions; coaching sessions may include others when relevant.

Support for developing perspective, purpose, and strategies is enhanced when working with partners, teams, and organizations. Group work dynamics include an interesting blend of individual preferences, group preferences, and interactions between group members. When clients learn together, individual preferences and goals interact to add complexity to coaching dynamics, especially related to facilitating discussions and strategy exploration. There is also great potential in between-session work and discussions, mutual accountability, as well as on-the-job support for applying strategies in the targeted environment.

The inherent power of group work is best realized by first acknowledging and navigating communication and interaction preferences with individual differences in mind. Coaches recognize that the client's experience and knowledge are their best way forward; an effective coach provides time for the client to reflect, process, and connect with feedback and new strategies. Often there are members of a partnership, group, or team who exist in different places on the continua of contributing and listening, deep and quick thinking, and other aspects of communication and development. These differences influence individual member's processing and willingness to contribute. When others are present in the coaching environment, the collective experience must be considered; measures must be taken to safeguard processing time and ensure social and psychological safety.

It is essential to determine methods proactively and collaboratively for team interactions based on preferences and purpose, while working toward common goals both collaboratively and as individual contributors. Setting group norms, recognizing how similarities and differences impact collaboration, and responding to the development needs of the team all provide means to optimize the experience of every team member. This is accomplished with conversations around expectations, possible tensions that may arise, processes for addressing needs, and how diverse preferences and talents will be supported in the group environment.

Develop flexible and fluent coaching skills for different needs and types of clients. Consider how topic development might be designed to meet the needs of the clients in Figure 1.2. How will psychological and emotional safety be safeguarded while encouraging development?

Individuals are complex; those with whom we work focus on development. They become aware of aspects of themselves and others and change to navigate the world more effectively. When you add one person to the coaching dynamic, each is referencing their own experience, experiences shared by the other, as well as their shared experience. To capture the increased complexity, consider the following factors and characteristics which influence the focus of the client groups in Figure 1.2.

Individual development levels: aware, engaged, empowered:

- Personal or professional development
- Self-selected or sponsored
- High potential or professional improvement plan
- Talent, adapt/transfer, or stretch goals

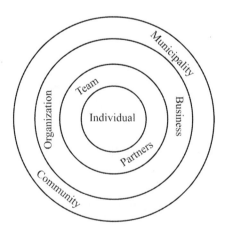

Figure 1.2 From the center each level includes prior level factors and adds another level of complexity. Illustration by the author.

Team adds complexity of interpersonal interactions:

- Partners or groups
- Social or professional relationships
- Same or complementary work
- Hierarchical or flat management
- Culture – ways of acting and interacting

Organization adds complexity of system:

- Whole organization or select members
- Group or individual facilitation
- Focus coaching or consulting
- For-profit or not-for-profit implications

Community adds complexity of competing, conflicting priorities:

- Select individuals, groups, members, and groups
- Common interests, preferences, geography, or culture
- Focus bridging gaps, collaboration, alignment, or diversifying
- Variety of structures and purposes exist together

A thoughtful approach to adapting strategies and questions to different clients and client types increases the effects of coaching. Working with individuals requires attention to affect, learning needs, goals, and energy levels. Clients who are leaders and who self-initiate development likely differ from those sponsored or on a professional improvement plan, including in terms of level of commitment, need, and buy-in. The complexity of client–coach dynamics increases exponentially when you are facilitating team development, or you are working with an entire organization with individuals in diverse roles who bring with them a variety of perspectives on coaching, development, and what is important. To hear authentic voices and create an effective environment, attend to developing norms for behaviors and explore strategies and skills such as *be curious* and *suspend judgment*.

Reflect and discuss

Fluency and flexibility:

1. In what aspects of coaching are you fluent? How did you become fluent?
2. How does your flexibility support work with individuals and in group settings?
3. What tenet(s) might you add for the special circumstances that arise when coaching a team or organization? How might you capture confidentiality or mutual expectations?

Perceptions

2

People perceive much in 20 seconds. In that time an individual may notice many of the innumerable elements in the scene surrounding them. Attention is drawn to an item, senses capture it and briefly store it for processing, working memory takes over by interacting with long-term memory to interpret and judge the sensory input. For efficiency, working memory chunks input for processing or connects meaning to the information. If it is not forgotten in the process and it is deemed relevant, information will be encoded to long-term memory. Then another feature is captured by the senses and similarly processed; senses constantly scan the environment.

Two people enter a room

Imagine the first day of beginners' watercolor class.

Charlie walks into the room and smells clay; it reminds them of something. Charlie describes the scene: There are about a dozen people in various conversations, looking at displays, and walking around the room. Most dress casually, comfortably, just like me. I scan the crowd, looking for a friend that should be here. I see them, as expected, scouting for a place to sit. I call, "Terry!"

Terry walks into the room and smells clay; it reminds them of something. Terry describes the scene: I see bright colors and am drawn to the large painting in the room around which there are several easels and stools. It seems I have my pick of workstation. There are two with a clear view of the large painting and they are easy to access. Charlie and I can sit together. I heard my name and turned to see Charlie heading toward me.

DOI: 10.4324/9781003332770-3

Charlie and Terry come together by the "best seats" and both exclaim, "The smell of clay!"

In a complex environment, the variability regarding what captures attention is great among individuals. Attention of senses is directed implicitly based on individual experience and preferences, processing is done without awareness, and much information is ignored or dismissed. What is noticed impacts thinking and behavior. The purpose of Perception Coaching® is to be increasingly aware of our thinking and actively assess perceptions so that we may interact more effectively with the environments, people, and roles in which we find ourselves involved.

Go to the scene and consider the perceptions of the people. Individuals in the room processed even the same aspects of the environment differently. Someone like Charlie is drawn to others; they likely scan for people they know, the instructor, or for friendly smiles. Someone feeling self-conscious may more intentionally observe others to judge if they are dressed appropriately for the class. With their focus on the people, they may not notice the arrangement of stools and easels in their first 20 seconds in the room.

Another student, Terry, immediately focuses on the art, stools, and easels with the purpose of finding the best seat for class. For them, that best seat may be front and center with a clear view of the instructor. Alternatively, they may strategically consider other factors. How clear is the path in and out of the seat? Where is the ventilation in the room? How many adjacent workstations are there to this seat? With their focus on finding their seat, they may not notice other people in the room, until a friend calls out to get their attention.

In writing, titles and headlines are separate and emphasized by size or font. Our perceptions guide thinking like an effective title. With our perceptions, attention is also drawn to the emphasized, including **bold**, LOUD, and novel things which our experience points to as interesting or unique and worthy of attention. Only with attention are senses engaged and aspects of the environment perceived or noticed. Our attention and senses are especially tuned to loud, unique, or interesting things for the important purpose of detecting possible danger.

Our preferences work as perceptual filters. When our eyes are drawn to a title, it is thought of as irrelevant or interesting, which causes one to dismiss it or dig deeper. Reading the first paragraph of an article to determine if it is of interest or use is akin to how our working memory serves us. Both steps include implicit processing which happens below the threshold of conscious thought. Finally, one may read the entire article and consider its implications, learning from the process; organizing knowledge is the role of long-term memory.

In search of a relevant focus, observers in an environment ignore or dismiss most present information in the first 20 seconds of experience thanks to the speed and efficiency of senses and working memory. The capacity of and preference for different senses varies by individual, contributing to perceptive variability; this is why several observers notice and remember different aspects of an environment or event.

The timeframe of 20 seconds is purposeful; it is a generous estimate of the time sensory data is stored before being lost or added to long-term memory. Sensed information stays in the *sensory register* for about one second and cognitive processing in working memory lasts about ten seconds. These numbers are rough estimates sufficient for an important point: the time spent analyzing data is brief; this does not align with the often-powerful implications individuals draw from their experiences. Seeing is believing; we should wonder about this when so much context is naturally missed.

The depth of processing varies, as well as the focus on what is processed. This leads observers to share an array of first impressions, which may make one question if the observers were in the same room. Implicit processing is continuous; in our first day of class example more information will be assessed as the student occupies the space. Data initially dismissed as irrelevant may be lost or ignored until attention is brought back to it directly or indirectly and it is revisited.

The capacity of each of our senses is essential to perception and processing, though capacity is not the only factor. Attention directs our senses starting with threat assessment, which is subjective and relative in nature. We may argue that both Terry and Charlie perceive threats differently, based on their initial focus. Terry may feel safe with a strategic location whereas Charlie relates to others in the room to feel safe. In this environment safety preferences are influenced primarily by psychological and emotional preferences.

Observing others to see if we dressed appropriately or looking at factors to determine the most strategic space indicates attention is on something relevant to us, sparking interactions between working and long-term memory. This is a more sustained process akin to reading more than the first paragraph of an article, though still likely done without explicit discernment which may lead to lost information. When further analysis of the sensed information leads to judgment that it misaligns with preferences or is not relevant to interests, or cognitive dissonance results in dismissal instead of inquiry, the information is lost.

Reflect and discuss

In writing, noticing starts with the attention-getter. The title, headline, or topic sentence is written not only for attention, but to indicate the subject of the writing.

1. What about the title informed your interests the most?
2. Which part of "Imagine your first day of beginners' watercolor class" cues a memory or idea for you? Have you had watercolor class, or an art class to which this is similar? Did you recently have a first day at work or school and experienced the optimism or apprehension of something new? How close is it to your experience?
3. If you were in the situation of the first day of beginning watercolor class, where would your attention go? Would you first scan the whole room, or is there a task you may first "investigate"?

Potential implications: Individual preferences influence how we mentally or physically interact with people, the painting, a familiar smell, where to sit, or other facets of the environment. In what ways or areas can this awareness support development?

Power and limits

The natural power of perception is the lever Perception Coaching® calls upon to support clients. Look more closely at the processes associated with perceptions. Perceptions are a mechanism which naturally develops and increases potential for survival. Senses first and foremost scan the environment searching for perceived threats to support physical safety. Perceptions also support identification of food and shelter. As we successfully navigate the world, perceptions are reinforced and may adapt; this iterative process continually runs in the background for our continued survival as we navigate the world.

Perceptions are implicitly developed and used without conscious thought; awareness of perceptions creates potential for life-enhancing reflection and development. The greatest potential exists in understanding and appreciating the complexity of preferences, diversity of experience, and how similarities and differences contribute to the most basic of needs, a sense of safety. Contemporary safety is markedly different than that of people living even a century ago. Societies have found ways to avoid and mitigate many high-fatality and physically dangerous threats. Though not a deep dive into the historic comparison of threats and how they have changed, the assertion is the focus of attention and perceptions must be shifted to address more commonly relevant safety concerns. Once addressed, the objective of perceptions can be directed from ensuring survival to actively flourishing.

Though many physical threats remain, issues of safety are often felt more subtly in the forms of psychological and emotional safety; people often sense risk related to expectations and judgments of others which may limit their future success. Additionally, the implicit, efficient generalizations for which perceptions are famous limit one's ability to see others as unique individuals. Finally, with safety at the core, our perceptions limit our ability to consider and pursue productive risks. Productive risk includes giving other individuals benefit of the doubt when we perceive they pose some sort of threat to us.

These safety preferences and inherent biases created when perceptual filters develop provide opportunities for Perception Coaching®. Because perceptual filters and preferences developed with limited experience and information, new perspectives given in a safe environment have great potential to create insight and change. Perceptions and preferences benefit from the intentional processing encouraged herein.

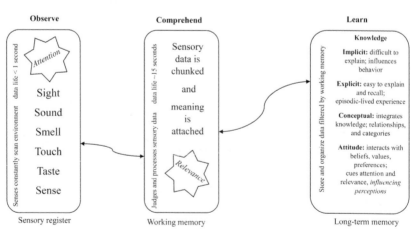

Figure 2.1 Perception to knowing process. Arrows indicate interactions between adjacent partners. Attention results in observations stored in the sensory register which interacts with working memory to comprehend the data; working memory interacts with knowledge in long-term memory which may result in the data being stored there. Illustration by the author.

Briefly described in Figure 2.1, the perception to knowing process provides a model to understand perceptual development as the result of interactions between our senses, preferences, and our capacity for understanding of the world. Generally, senses attend to features of the environment, working memory interprets the information by interacting with long-term memory, then long-term memory stores it, further developing our preferences and understanding of the world. For convenience we label these steps *observation*, *comprehension*, and *learning*. Next, we will explore what each of the information processing steps involves.

Process and potential

The processes associated with perceptions are often illustrated as data moving through separate storage areas, the influences of attention and capacity dictating what data are saved and lost.

Observation: Sensory registers and attention

The information gathered by our senses is thought to be represented in the same form in which it was sensed. Iconic, echoic, olfactory, haptic, and gustatory memories are stored in the sensory register as observed (sight, sound, smell, touch, and taste, respectively). This means visual data exist as they are seen, sound data as they are heard, and data similarly exist for smell, touch, and taste while in the sensory register. The volume of data available to be sensed is extremely large, far more than perceptual capabilities can process (Barlow, 1961).

Theoretically, the memory of a sensed stimulus is not processed at any level in the registry and only endures in the registry for a second, less than a second when there are many items competing for attention during continual scanning. Early research in which participants recall stimuli that should be stored in the sensory register gives us our one second estimate of time spent in the registry. Research done in this way provides a bit of a confound, as asking leads to consideration of the sense data, immediately moving it to working memory, making it difficult to pinpoint why or when sense data fades. Iconic sensory register data memory and fading can be observed anecdotally by attaching a light to a string and swinging it in circles in the dark; the circle of light you "see" is the result of the sensory memory of the light when it occupied places along the circle it traveled. Similarly, if you are listening to someone speaking and your attention waivers, when your attention returns, you will remember a word or two from before your attention returned, because the word or two was still in the echoic register.

The sensory register has capacity to store all sensory data simultaneously in the form sensed. The short life of sensory information in a register with great capacity may initially seem contradictory. In most environments innumerable stimuli of multiple types are observed. Short retention allows one to continuously update sense data, to scan and take in new aspects of surroundings without getting bogged down. Replacement or overwriting help explain the short duration of sense information in this holding space. Continuous scanning is especially useful in new, complex environments when comfort and threat avoidance are relevant; these needs have significant implications for perceptions and preferences we explore more in upcoming sections.

Attention

Attention is the selective, primary director of our senses. Without attention, we do not sense information about the environment. We may look at or hear something and not register it, if our attention is elsewhere, it goes unnoticed. The limited capacity of attention is well documented; great variation in capacity exists between individuals and within individuals across environments.

What gets attention is as varied as individual differences regarding capacity to attend to a given number of environmental features. Because attention is limited, our perceptions about what is relevant direct our senses; things are missed that are not understood or seen as relevant by one's perceptual filter. Relevant and interesting are preferential constructs; information judged as such is stored and developed in long-term memory.

Forrest et al. (2022) noted existing research showed when threat- and goal-relevant stimuli were presented simultaneously, attention prioritized those that were goal-relevant. To further understanding, they manipulated the presentation of stimuli to occur in different stages of attentional processing with similar results. The exception: attention to temporary goals over threat was reduced in people who expressed feeling more anxiety. Safety is the evolutionary default, survival is the goal of attention in the implicit working of the mind. Explicitly setting goals is a powerful means to direct attention, to move its purpose beyond safety to providing the mind information which supports flourishing. The interaction between attention and preferences will be discussed further in working and long-term memory.

Comprehension and working memory

Some refer to working memory as the central processor; it reaches into the sensory register for things to process and interacts with long-term memory to judge the things as worthy of retention. One way to understand the mechanics and limitations of working memory is to display a string of numbers or nonsense syllables for a short time and then test recall. Most people can work with five to nine items at a time, chunking them for expediency, before they start losing items when they attempt to recall them. Active processing can focus attention and keep the senses actively engaged with observation; this is explicit processing, done by verbalizing or adding context. Verbal or mental rehearsal creates a path to recall which becomes stronger with practice. Even this type of manipulation includes interactions with long-term memory to allow working memory to chunk or attach meaning to the data. These processes create connections for remembering the information.

All processing introduces personal interpretation as encoding begins, altering both the form and meaning of the information which started as sensory data. Two individuals observing the same thing likely have different perspectives on it due to personal interpretations. Furthermore, when the data is judged to be irrelevant it is dismissed and lost, or if the data cannot be processed effectively, because it is lost due to capacity or time, this increases the potential difference in understanding between observers.

Relevance, interpretation, and encoding

The interactions between working memory and long-term memory focus on sense-making; this is frequently done implicitly, automatically, below conscious thought. When an item is processed by working memory, it is compared with existing knowledge in long-term memory. Similarities, patterns, and relationships are quickly determined and encoded for long-term memory. If it is deemed relevant, the new knowledge is added to memory. Sometimes new information conflicts with existing knowledge; the result can be "mislearning" in many forms including dismissing the conflicting information as nonsense or distorting the conflicting information so that it better aligns with existing knowledge, creating misconceptions. The best outcome is learning, which includes revising naïve ideas or replacing existing problematic knowledge. The potential for drawing inappropriate conclusions or "mislearning" during implicit processing is great, as we will discuss in long-term memory and more deeply as we explore preference and perception.

Perception check strategies

Goal: Question implicit thinking, increase curiosity, and enable positive emotions

Efforts: Suspend judgment, practice metacognition, seek perspective, resilient learning

Perception check strategies are especially beneficial to counter the implicit evolutionary focus on risk aversion, leveraging the power of goals. Set goals to find things for which to be grateful, identify people to compliment, and recognize one's achievements to also increase the productive, positive bias to support well-being. These strategies are also supportive when anticipating or facing conflict, strong emotions are present, and mixed feelings exist around an experience or event.

1. *Get curious* about what is known and how it is known. **Ask yourself:**

   - What do I **know**? For what is there certainty?
   - How do I know it?

   a. Evidence/history/experience – **check for:**

      i. overgeneralization
      ii. correlation taken as cause
      iii. dismissed counterexamples
      iv. biases of sources.

   b. Attitude/gut/intuition

      i. What emotion accompanies the knowledge?
      ii. May this knowledge be a belief or opinion?

   c. Other?

      i. What other ways of knowing inform you?
      ii. Do they naturally lead to generative questions or judgment?

2. *Reflect* to examine lived experience and accompanying thought processes by noticing:

   a. how the experience was sensed and felt
   b. how one interacted in the experience or while observing the event
   c. metacognition

      i. *what* and *how* one was thinking
      ii. *why* one focused there.

3. *Seeking* aims to discover misunderstandings and alternatives by noticing:

    a. What alternative interpretations, views, motivations, experience, purpose, expectations may exist?
    b. What conclusions were drawn or reinforced?
    c. What information may be missing or could be explored to better understand another perspective?

4. *Set a goal* to increase perceptual awareness of productive features, such as I **will:**

    •   look for and appreciate diverse talents
    •   notice more opportunities
    •   sense the good in every interaction.

5. *Process with a thought partner or complementary friend* who can provide feedback, an alternative perspective, or interpretation. A journal project, electronic messaging, or otherwise explicitly processing the results of implicit processing provides perspective.

Perception check strategies increase one's ability to check biases, see alternative interpretations, be curious, and suspend judgment. As an intervention, it is most effective near the time of the event, or during, if practical. Immediacy increases the opportunity to sense dismissed or misunderstood features and consider alternatives beyond those naturally sensed.

Learning and long-term memory

The role of long-term memory is to build a store of organized, integrated knowledge which supports safe navigation in the world. It does this, for the most part, implicitly. Much of the knowledge which directs behavior may be difficult to explain. One may explain it by saying I go with my gut, I just know it, that is just the way it is, everyone knows that, or with similar nonspecific, yet vehemently valued, explanations. Something you "just know" is more accurately described as something learned naturally through experience. Your information processing system was working implicitly, without active monitoring, and you are operating with the results unaware of the source and how it came to be *knowledge*. Information that has not been examined consciously in "the light of day" may create tensions, biases, or have other subtle implications.

That is not to say implicitly derived knowledge is misinformation; it may be useful and productive knowledge which will become more meaningful when examined for accuracy and intention. Confidence in our natural learning processes, or more importantly the knowledge they produce, can inhibit our growth. Experiential knowledge is valued above other types as "evidence" of a phenomenon, corroborated by those who *will believe it when they see it.* Individual preferences direct attention to provide sensory data for processing which then contributes to our knowledge. The interaction between preferences and knowledge is naturally reinforcing and limiting. To understand this interaction, we will explore two aspects: how we categorize and relate information, and how information that contradicts well-developed personal theories is likely processed.

Types of knowledge

Episodic memory is different than much of the information used to categorize, group, and understand information. Episodic memories are those which include first-hand experience; those immersive experiences recalled by the participant or witness. These memories and related knowledge, stored as mental models or schema, are given preference in the face of contradiction and have higher "stickiness" than information from other sources. Validity of interpretations, conclusions, and the memory itself is rarely questioned. Episodic memories inform *personal theories*, integral aspects of mental models which are borne of the informal learning that naturally occurs while interpreting experience. Processing personal theories to reach conclusions may be explicit, using facts drawn from *semantic memory*, though much of the information was likely perceived, categorized, and interpreted implicitly, unavoidably filtered and magnified by the biases of individual preferences. Conclusions related to personal theories are robust, *I saw it with my own eyes,* though the evidence and perspective is limited and biased by preferences.

Conceptual knowledge relates multiple ideas which may be imagined as a network of data that relates actions (procedural knowledge) appropriately to features and conditions (declarative knowledge). If we know a procedure and we apply it and get the result we want, we conclude that that procedure works in that circumstance. If this result is overgeneralized, a by-product of confirmation bias, it creates misinformation in episodic memory. Reasoning and interpretation around the results may also create false dichotomies, logical fallacies, and overgeneralizations. Episodic information and misinformation are stored as knowledge that references lived experience. Unlearning or replacing misinformation is significantly more difficult than adding new accurate knowledge or integrating new related knowledge.

Yan et al. (2016) studied learners' conceptions of inductive learning and found that though learning integrated topics is superior to blocked learning by topic, learners believed the opposite was true. Even in the face of evidence from both experience-based and theory-based techniques, the misconceptions held. It was determined that the robustness of the misconception was due to three factors: a sense of topic fluency in block learning, pre-existing beliefs about integrated learning, and eagerness to believe that their learning was special – perhaps integrated learning works best for many, just not me. As was seen in that study, the number of factors that help solidify personal theories creates a barrier to dislodging misconceptions.

Confirmation bias is developed when a phenomenon is detected and the initial conclusion is formed; senses then detect evidence which supports the initial conclusion, and the memory stores it; if new evidence does not agree with the initial conclusion, the data is often dismissed as an anomaly or "the exception that proves the rule." If confirming information is evident, regardless of its significance, certainty about the initial conclusion grows, regardless of how much contradictory evidence exists. Coaching supports recognizing mislearning and developing stable, meaningful learning. Coaching conversations and questions often create opportunities to challenge misconceptions and explore related blind spots.

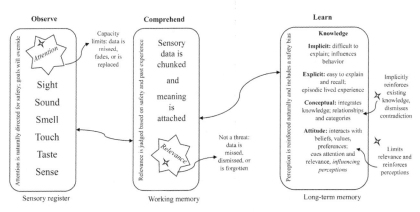

Figure 2.2 The limits of the Figure 2.1 perception to knowing process are highlighted. The starred concepts become opportunities for Perception Coaching®. Illustration by the author.

Paying attention to perception brings meaningful insights which help clients see more possibilities and ways to support their mission, vision, and goals around well-being, productivity, and innovation. Coaches facilitate this process by first supporting clients' understanding of their existing perceptual filters and how they interact with information processing, with a focus on their goal area. Together we explore and evaluate perspectives and strategies that are interesting to the client and relevant to the client's goals. This exploration is an ideal time to introduce Perception Check strategies with a clear focus on their goal. Finally, steps and procedures for implementation are set for strategies which align with preferences and have potential for goal progress. With help from the coach, the client selects their personal experiments to adjust and enhance their personal theories. This process, paired with a focus on continuous development, guides perceptual shifts which support improved well-being and success.

Learning with purpose

Brains are adept at solving puzzles; seeking answers and solutions is a primary human goal. The attention to risk as a default is displaced by setting goals beyond survival. When individuals set goals, their attention is implicitly drawn to things and information sensed as relevant to the goals. Integration space is established in long-term memory to store challenges, wonderings, complex concepts, ambiguity, ideas which cause dissonance, and disparate interesting knowledge that may be useful one day. It is best established mentally, though like other important things, physical representations such as lists, graphic organizers, or pictures support establishing and maintaining an integration space in long-term memory. The integration space strategies support seeing more by intentionally increasing the number of things considered relevant, so that less information is dismissed and lost.

Arguably, there are few things worse than a chronic challenge; there is no satisfaction of solution or completion. A challenge is like building a puzzle and discovering there are pieces missing. Completing the puzzle is supported by the goal to find missing pieces, which creates a means to sense more in the environment. While constructing the puzzle attention was on the collection of pieces on the tabletop; when it is realized a piece is missing, attention broadens to more of the tabletop, under any items on the table, and under the table itself. When one holds a complex goal the need to process more of the environment is also encouraged. Information is held a little longer as working memory interacts with long-term memory, and attention is drawn to more features of the environment or resource to increase the possibility of connecting information with the goal.

When one remains mindful of complex interests and ideas using the integration space strategies, new learning is regularly checked against its contents. Comparisons and connections are made as the new idea interacts with the stored interests and concepts and one determines how the new idea supports, connects, causes tension, or provides insight into existing knowledge. This process reinforces the new knowledge, enhances existing knowledge, and creates new connections among concepts making ideas more accessible and understanding more robust.

As a teacher and graduate student my focus was mathematics education and the missing pieces many students faced related to number sense, always seeking situations or activities in which misconceptions or gaps may originate. To investigate misunderstandings, puzzle representations, computation, algorithms, units, quantitative contexts, and conceptual development are kept in mind, existing in my math integration space. Revisiting ideas or learning new ideas prompts reflection on the ever-present goal of accessible mathematics.

Early in my teaching career, when revisiting Howard Garner's theory of multiple intelligences, I used this focus to consider the impact of the theory on learning modes. Educators strategically work to address different ways of thinking using the gradual release teaching method: show an example, work together, and then work independently on similar exercises. This strategy relies on selecting the best example, highlighting the most instructive student ideas, and recognizing when learners are ready to practice independently.

Intelligence theories suggested learner comprehension should be the center of planning to support efficiently sharing the right content; this improves learner outcomes. Diverse student needs make every step of the gradual release process a place of potential for access or to introduce misunderstanding. With further processing and reflection, connections evolved and influenced my exploration of how different learning processes complement different types of mathematical knowledge. An example of this includes procedural knowledge, often favored in early grades when computation is the focus. Limiting understanding of computation to learning steps creates barriers when more abstract concepts are introduced after the basic procedures are established. Traditionally in primary school learners experienced subtraction problems which were modeled, discussed, and practiced creating simple rules: when subtracting the smaller number is always "taken away from" the larger number and when writing a subtraction equation, the larger number comes first. Oversimplification causes confusion later when integers are introduced and in fractions when larger numbers in the denominator often represent a smaller quantity. The over-simplified "rules" for this procedure lead to over-generalizations which contribute to numerous mathematical misconceptions.

The interaction of student preferences, multiple intelligences, and content provides a multifaceted approach to planning which creates an environment for the conceptual development of mathematics. Rather than oversimplify, over time use accurate language, explore relationships, and share multiple representations and modes accessible to other ways of knowing to effectively support mathematical contexts beyond efficiently applying algorithms and other procedural knowledge. As I explore and integrate new ideas, such as representation via analogies, mathematics knowledge is recalled, revised, and connected to other disciplines.

A current complex puzzle existing in my integration space is that of effective communication. It is connected to teaching mathematics, as mathematics is communication specifically focused on quantity. In addition to topics involved in mathematics, my integration space includes questions to ponder. For communication these questions resurface in different contexts, for each asking questions such as: What is the purpose of communication? For whom is communication intended? What means of communication are preferred? How does one navigate between transparency and overcommunicating? How may individuals' content schema influence related communication. When is it better to be clear? When may ambiguity better support intention? When integration space houses both topics of interest and interesting questions more information captures your attention. The cost and benefit of maintaining integration space is potential interference regarding efficiency in implicit processing, compared to when the focus was on threat reduction. Individuals tend to seek a comfortable balance between threat assessment and acceptable risk, and these should be explored; individual capacities, preferences, and needs determine the utility of the integration space strategy.

Walk through the integration space strategies with effective communication in mind or explore your own missing puzzle pieces.

Reflect and discuss

1. What information gets remembered, and why?
2. How might one support attention when processing complex environments?
3. How might exploring their own perceptions challenge a client?
4. Some cite that their knowledge comes from the school of hard knocks – what might this indicate about their perceptions or perceptual filter?

Client focus   **3**

Coaches serve clients for a variety of reasons, often with the common denominator of striving to reach higher potential; this challenge requires exploration, effort, and evaluation. Clients may come to coaching with a development perspective in mind; their perspective may not be formalized, only sensed. One may say, *my youngest child left home and I... want to effectively transition... pay more attention to my needs... want to learn something new.* Meeting worthwhile challenges requires effective goals, perspective development, productive risks, learning from mistakes, and persistence over time.

Clarify coaching goals

Anticipating the first visit with a new or potential client is intense. Their goals, needs, and approaches are things one cannot anticipate, though one tries. Coaches strive to add value, be of service, and optimize time together with clients, starting with little context. This resource provides tools to understand and support clients, from generating questions to understand clients' talents, needs, and goals, to techniques to explore and address common client development needs. "What brings you to coaching?" is a great place to start your first visit with a client and may be all you need to start the journey of understanding and supporting their efforts.

Clients' stories provide insight to a lifetime of successes, learning, and natural development of perceptions, as well as personal attitudes and current world views. To coach with perceptions in mind means recognizing existing perspectives and acknowledging the value and limits a client's current

DOI: 10.4324/9781003332770-4

perceptual filters contribute to their life. In this book, the topics of well-being, productivity, and innovation provide context for applying the key strategies of Perception Coaching®. Through exploration of these goal topics, readers develop processes which focus coaching efforts on checking perceptions, seeking knowledge, and prioritizing growth. For each topic explore its factors within the context of the learning progression, taking the topic from developing awareness, to increasing engagement, and finally to empower clients to find success in the topic areas relevant to them.

So far, Part 1 has described the coaching model and provided a structured progression of content for a new coach. The content started by exploring coaching approaches, then understanding perceptions, and we have now reached client goals. These main ideas include aspects which add detail to develop depth of understanding as well as connect the ideas to practice.

Parts 2 and 3 are organized with topics which focus on clients' coaching goals. A coach may create a program with the objective of developing awareness from well-being through innovation, focusing on each of the main branches. In this case clients' development would progress from expanding self-knowledge to navigating life with others, onto being more productive, and finally finding ways to innovate; this is a learning continuum in which each new concept builds complexity and depth of understanding.

Fluency in navigating topics is recommended because it is likely that individual client stories will indicate that early coaching conversations focus on an area other than *sense of self*. When clients tell stories, listen for awareness to appropriately focus on any of the goal topics herein. When you connect their story to one of the three big topics, this is your opportunity to become curious about their current level of development; listen for indications of engagement and empowerment.

For instance, a new client may describe how they journal and reflect daily and state that they want to use their talents to innovate. Starting a coaching conversation with this client focused on sense of self will likely frustrate them, even though it may benefit and inform you, as their coach. The goal the client indicates, using their talents for innovation, is your best starting point. Ask them about the talents they would like to use and the opportunities for innovation that they sense. The same client may later indicate a belief or preference that is a barrier – then it makes sense to explore that aspect of self in the coaching conversation. Ensure the coaching conversation revolves around the client's goal, their context, and their responses to your authentic questions to effectively support their efforts; the experiences they describe are appreciated and valued, as these are the primary sources that inform coaching actions.

The progression and integration of topics within Parts 2 and 3 of this resource are designed to support your ability to locate and respond to clients flexibly, with information or strategies from any section based on their immediate interests and needs.

Bias box

Theories of development

The most practical development theory to coaching is Journey, as it encourages growth without age or needs having undue influence.

Lane et al. (2019, p. 369) describe three learning theories which are especially impactful to client development for different coaching approaches and goals:

Phase Theory – Learning has chronological phases dependent on cultural context. *Experience counts* is a phrase that can reflect the wisdom gained through different phases of life.

Transition coaches may find this theory type useful and wish to research the following theorists: Charlotte Buhler, Carl Jung, Daniel Levinson, and Bernice Neugarten.

Stage Theory – Learning focuses on basic needs, followed by belonging, then more abstract needs. Those who refer to Maslow's needs when determining goals may benefit from a stage approach.

Well-being coaches may want to investigate these theorists: Carol Gilligan, Robert Kegan, Lawrence Kohlbergh, and Jean Piaget.

Journey Theory – Learning begins with naïve, simple thinking and evolves to more complex and dynamic thinking as learners make decisions. Curiosity and life experiences are key to journeys.

Mentoring coaches can learn more by exploring the works of Laurent Daloz with his perspective of educational and mentoring journeys and William Perry's intellectual and ethical development.

You may detect parallels in the brief descriptions of these theoretical approaches; those are likely due to this author's bias. Clients' efforts toward goals benefit from their coach's expertise in development to inform next steps as well as the sustained attention coaching encourages.

Even briefly exploring relevant theorists, their perspectives, and their interpretations provides insights which improve clarity regarding how they resonate with different coaching perspectives as well as your ability to adapt coaching approaches when you encounter barriers to client development.

Self-assess

Which theory resonates with your coaching approach? For each pair mark the strength of your preference between the two anchors; the center is neutral, indicating no preference.

Phase ---- 3 ---- 2 ---- 1 ---- 0 ---- 1 ---- 2 ---- 3 ---- Stage
Phase ---- 3 ---- 2 ---- 1 ---- 0 ---- 1 ---- 2 ---- 3 ---- Journey
Journey ---- 3 ---- 2 ---- 1 ---- 0 ---- 1 ---- 2 ---- 3 ---- Stage

Note the order and strength of your preferences.

Reflect and discuss

Consider the purpose, values, and benefits of the three theories:

1.   Describe circumstances or content for which each is most useful:

   •   Phase – informed by age and culture
   •   Stage – similar to Maslow's hierarchy
   •   Journey – going from simple to complex

2.   These three development theories are not comprehensive; what perspectives would you add?
3.   How does this content contribute to your coaching perspective?

Types of reasoning

Clients regularly reason, are reasonable, and can be reason seekers; understanding client preferences and talents as reasoners facilitates one's ability to listen and respond in ways that are accessible to the client, resonate with them, and support their development.

Reasoning is essential to development and includes different ways of thinking which bridge a multitude of different needs with relevant solutions. Reasoning is the metaphorical bridge between perception and comprehension, knowing and doing, tension and relief, complexity and understanding, or opportunity and plan. Recognize how one reasons and barriers to reasoning to increase coaching efficacy, and to bolster connections which lead to improved understanding and commitment.

Analogical reasoning connects different items using similarity, for instance hours relate to time and decibels relate to sound. These statements are analogous because in each pair the first item is a measurement unit of the second. Analogies can also be quite abstract. One may be hiking down a nature trail and sense the activity as being *similar to* completing a project at work, noting that each takes dedicated time to finish. Analogies are especially intriguing when they link disparate ideas, and one discovers increasingly deep alignment between the two ideas.

Nature trails and projects at work each have places in which an individual may be diverted, which may enhance the experience or cause one to be lost or go off task. Shortcuts exist in both trails and projects, which may make the path more efficient or may lead to missing key features. Analogical reasoning is especially useful to provide context when explaining new information that may be complex, linking the new information to contexts to which the learner can relate.

Inductive reasoning leverages pattern recognition and completion. It is used to respond to a prompt like "given a sequence, what may be the next thing or missing element?" Inductive reasoning focuses on order of rank, size, degree, time, or other relative attributes. Inductive reasoning is the approach used for identifying preferences and priorities, such as which projects are the most enjoyable and which projects are most important.

Strategies to improve inductive reasoning may include brainstorming possibilities for analysis or identifying attributes of a given group of items, depending on if the struggle is related to determining rank order or pattern elements, for example. Developing procedural knowledge is done using effective inductive reasoning to recognize ordinal relationships between multiple steps in a process. When a client faces a barrier, coaches may ask, *what is missing or out of order?* to identify needs or missed steps.

Deductive reasoning is in many ways the opposite of inductive; the goal is to eliminate alternatives that don't meet the criteria. Logic puzzles illustrate and develop deductive reasoning; often a grid is provided as a graphic organizer for these puzzles with nouns on one axis and descriptors on the other. The goal of deduction in a logic problem is to match each noun with the correct descriptor based on clues. The puzzler eliminates alternatives with each clue and as matches are made, until all nouns have one and only one matching descriptor.

Doyle's character Sherlock Holmes was a master of deduction, using clues to eliminate the impossible to discover the true solution. When faced with several alternatives, a coaching question that leverages deductive reasoning is *which is not the best way to proceed?*

Cause and effect reasoning is used to discover or explain dependency relationships. There are many speakers who share the actions and thinking that made them successful, and yet few others seem able to take that information and replicate the success. Anyone experienced in statistics likely recognizes that *correlation does not imply causation*; there must be reasonable evidence of one being prerequisite for the other to occur. Individuals often attribute a result to an event that also happened in the same timeframe; they remember that these two things occurred together in the past and conclude there is a cause–effect relationship. Dispelling or exploring a problematic connection is complex and key to improved reasoning.

Understanding cause and effect relationships relevant to a goal supports creating effective plans for success. Coaches help check perceptions regarding cause–effect reasoning to ensure confirmation bias is not contributing to the conclusion. When a client describes an apparent cause–effect relationship, encourage reflection. The reasoning required to collect the appropriate evidence to determine a cause–effect relationship is useful in coaching and reasoning. Because personal theories are reinforced in implicit processing, ask the client to think of a time the two things may not or did not happen together. If probing further, ask if there is a specific person or place where the two things don't occur together.

Given the right prompt and time, individuals will see coincidence and correlation for what they are, and only attribute causation with sufficient evidence and logical reasoning. Are you curious about this type of reasoning? Search using the phrase "correlation does not imply causation" to discover examples of unrelated things that correlate. You will find silly and surprising examples; these help to illustrate the type of reasoning required to debunk or confirm cause and effect relationships.

Categorical reasoning or grouping requires flexible thinking as it is purpose driven. Categories may be mutually exclusive, there may exist relationships between or among them such as in a hierarchy or family, and categories may be defined for convenience. Kitchen items are often stored in drawers near where they are used or by how they are used; eating, serving, stovetop, baking, and other functional labels support kitchen drawer organization. Many households also categorize one drawer as a catch all or junk drawer, a place in which items that do not clearly fit existing categories reside. Regardless of the purpose, reasoning related to grouping requires understanding a variety of things about the items to be categorized. To group items, one compares and contrasts multiple characteristics, recognizes relationships among the items, and judges the significance of each trait and relationship for the purpose of categorization. Categorization includes complex thinking which often requires support.

Clients often benefit from creating lists to identify preferences or priorities, as described in inductive reasoning; categorization is a reasoning approach that can support these purposes. When determining preferences, the list may be sorted into categories such as *always important, sometimes important,* and *never important.* An arguably lesser reasoning skill, examining part–whole relationships, may support prioritization of groups. For instance, in a card sort activity if one sorts "well-being" into always important, then when considering "fitness" one may reason using part–whole relationships. If fitness is thought of as a facet of well-being, perhaps it also belongs in the always important category. This also avoids a perceived contradiction that may result if well-being is always important, and fitness is sometimes important; alternatively, that may be the case if one's fitness is not considered an essential part of one's well-being.

To summarize, consider reasoning types when barriers to decision-making, prioritization, or other strategic thinking goals are present. Judgment is key to reasoning as a skill; when a decisive trait is identified or when there is a close call, explore the reasoning that relates to the decision; explicit processing builds confidence and consistency regarding reasoning. Perceptive individuals with excellent reasoning skills benefit from thinking about their thinking.

Confirmation bias and other implicit processes can derail intentions to be more thoughtful in certain contexts. In times when one is overburdened, stressed, sleep deprived, hungry, or suffering from numerous other distractions, capacity for reasoning is negatively impacted. Developing reasoning requires accurate explicit knowledge as well as purpose, awareness, energy, and cognitive capacity; addressing each of these factors improves reasoning skills. The first step to elevate thinking is to be aware of how much work brains do without overt processing. Then, engage in metacognition, thinking about thinking. By monitoring what we think we expand how we think, and more productive thinking habits develop. Finally, empower thinking by setting goals and actions for productive thinking. These three steps also happen to describe the Perception Coaching® development progression used to support growth.

Levels of understanding

The aware-engaged-empowered cycle briefly described to elevate thinking is an adaptable learning path for conceptual development. Use the cycle to support clients' efforts to explore topics related to their goals, identify relevant factors, build competencies, create plans to face challenges, and accomplish goals with their experience and expertise in mind. The three levels provide an iterative sequence, which repeats whenever new aspects of concepts are discovered or found relevant.

Awareness is the developmental introduction to new ideas, perspectives, or approaches and is especially relevant when those have potential to support goals. Given a new concept, one must first be aware of occurrences of the idea or phenomenon; then initiation to the topic occurs and explicit knowledge and understanding are developed. Time is spent sensing characteristics, definitions, clarity, and other perspectives in this phase. Questions which focus on this level include prompts to sense, observe, and identify how and when the topic occurs, its traits, and its relevance. Ask *what*, *what else*, or *why* questions to support reflection, exploration, and learning.

Engagement is the process of fluency development regarding a topic. When engaged, one applies and practices the ideas developed through awareness. There may be barriers to using knowledge in integration or application; engagement includes finding and navigating the right path in exploration, as well as evaluating relevant skills and strategies related to a topic. Questions that focus on this level include prompts to reflect on past success, assess needs, and resilience when encountering challenges; ask *how* or *when* questions to support planning, experiments, and other actions.

Empowerment occurs when concept expertise develops and is a source of progress and hope. This is characterized by observed potential, when ways to implement, adapt, or transfer a tool or strategy is sensed and one is compelled to pursue change. When facing barriers to change and innovation related to the topic, questions to progress on this level prompt curiosity and creativity, drawing from and combining diverse strategies; ask *what if* questions to support vision and hypotheses creation, consider alternatives, and manage risk.

To illustrate, imagine a client's focus is on developing social connections. A coaching conversation leads to awareness that connections start with bids for attention. Between sessions the client explores this by identifying different types of bids, noticing when they are appropriate, and observing the variability of how different individuals reach out and respond. The client discovers glances and other body language that had gone unnoticed, and that they prefer to share a glance and nod and experience varying results with this type of bid. The client then engages in practice to sense when to use different bids and which bids feel most authentic. When application is understood, empowerment is experienced at a mixer or networking event where meaningful connections are made using and watching for bids for attention.

Bias box

Levels of understanding

Awareness must be cultivated because what we sense, think, and do naturally influences understanding and development without being subjected to scrutiny.

Levels of understanding benefit both client perspective and development. When one is aware of or has a goal regarding an aspect of their world, they can then engage with it to develop knowledge and expertise to determine potential for its use. Without explicit awareness implicit cognitive processes evaluate and limit access to sensory and other dismissed data. Aware, engaged, empowered describes a developmental cycle useful for a variety of concepts and strategies.

Aware: Perceptive filters implicitly limit what is noticed, so that the environment can be efficiently processed. Awareness is a means to introduce new ideas, perspectives, or approaches and is especially relevant when previously unnoticed ideas have potential to support goals.

Developing awareness includes seeking examples of the idea in life, noticing related ideas, and building understanding of the idea from information which had previously been ignored or taken for granted.

Engaged: Fluency development happens when there is engagement focused on the idea. Engagement also includes immersion in the moment, when the application and practice of ideas developed through awareness occurs.

When one is engaged, one interacts with the focus idea for extended time and with effect; both attention and cognition target aspects of the idea to enhance related understanding and application.

Empowered: Expertise is a source of progress and hope; ways to implement, adapt, or transfer a tool or strategy are sensed and one advocates for or pursues change. Empowerment includes confidence that application efforts around the idea contribute to make meaningful progress toward a goal.

When one is empowered they are motivated to adapt and apply ideas that may pose some risk, optimistic that greater gains will occur.

Self-assess

What level is your focus when developing understanding for most topics or ideas? For each pair mark the strength of your preference between the two anchors; the center is neutral, indicating no preference.

Aware ---- 3 ---- 2 ---- 1 ---- 0 ---- 1 ---- 2 ---- 3 ---- Engaged
Aware ---- 3 ---- 2 ---- 1 ---- 0 ---- 1 ---- 2 ---- 3 ---- Empowered
Empowered ---- 3 ---- 2 ---- 1 ---- 0 ---- 1 ---- 2 ---- 3 ---- Engaged

Note the order and strength of your preferences.

Reflect and discuss

Consider the purpose, values, and benefits of the three steps:

1. Describe circumstance or content for which each is most useful:
   - Awareness of ideas or strategies
   - Applying or practicing
   - Pursuing expertise

2. The levels of development appear to be sequential, with awareness being first. Describe a situation in which following this sequence may not be useful.

3. How does this content contribute to your coaching perspective?

Understanding development levels supports creating points for checking understanding or knowledge when challenges arise. For example, when someone engaged in a process is asked to implement it faster, they may eliminate an important step. This results in understanding that they are not aware of why the step is in place. If their development started with learning how to do a process, they likely do not know why they are doing each part of the process. Focusing on how is efficient to get someone started working and they may become fluent with practice, but developing expertise will be difficult. Gaps in knowledge created by unawareness limit one's ability to respond to unexpected circumstances or results the way someone with expertise can.

New math is an idea which demonstrates this. Traditionally in schools, algorithms functioned as learners' introduction to computation. This makes sense as evaluation of student performance regarding computational algorithms is straightforward because there is often a single correct way to answer, and errors can be easily detected. The opportunity to introduce error occurs in each step, particularly when multiple lines and columns are required, such as in multi-digit multiplication or division. Another caution, because the processes were introduced first, many learners experienced a disconnect with context and therefore struggled with application. Even when students could do well with computation, if the results were not meaningful to them they could not effectively apply the process to solve problems presented as a narrative in word problems or real-world scenarios.

The frequency of errors in computation using multi-step algorithms resulted in adaptations such as lattice multiplication and scaffold division. Pushback was often the result when these new procedures were brought home because many caregivers learned traditional algorithms and did not recognize the parallels between the related methods. An objective of new math is to move learning from procedural to conceptual development of mathematical knowledge, which is a shift from the focus of computation in primary grades. Conceptual development is more gradual and requires learning and exploration as whole numbers, fractions, integers, and other representations are introduced in the context of computation.

To leverage the learning cycle, first determine your clients' familiarity with the useful topic or perspective. How do they talk about it? What do they know? What have they tried? What do they hope to accomplish?

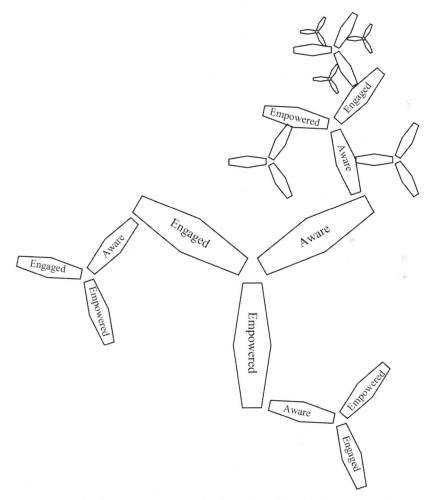

Figure 3.1 The largest iteration is the fractal seed and indicates a goal area with branches representing the aware, engage, and empower levels of development. The pattern continues along the levels of development as learning occurs through exploration. Illustration by the author.

Through exploration evolution occurs, moving naturally from becoming aware, to becoming engaged, to becoming empowered regarding concepts and processes of interest. As we seek expertise, we identify or become aware of aspects of the idea, then we can become engaged in practicing or understanding the idea, which provides insights to ways the power of the idea supports our efforts. The explore, engage, empower model leverages the notion that as knowledge of a topic develops, one becomes aware of more aspects related to the topic, which in turn develops depth of understanding for the topic in a repeating pattern representing the growth one realizes while developing expertise. This may be mapped or planned as shown in Figure 3.1. Growth is not uniform and should be intentionally directed to meet client needs.

The iterative process of sensing, interacting with, and leveraging concepts and strategies with increasing depth and detail is the seed process for the framework which supports our efforts to map detailed aspects of expertise regarding goal topics.

Note on intentional repetition: When navigating or designing a complex system, recurring design elements provide structure which supports deep understanding. The pattern applied to the Perception Coaching® model is a three-branch fractal; branches are labeled with three primary goal areas: well-being, productivity, and innovation. Using this model, one lives with the ambiguity of having three branches that simultaneously represent three discrete topics for which we strive to develop from aware to empowered, while these topics have potential ordinality as well as other connections among them. Ordinality is seen when well-being is a precursor to productivity, which in turn is a precursor to innovation. Alternatively, the developmental order of topics may be perceived in this manner: one benefits from being *aware of* well-being, *engaged in* productivity, and *empowered by* innovation.

People do not develop evenly across disciplines, or even within concepts. One may be interested in productivity and find pursuing the paths of well-being, detailed in Figure 3.2, to be especially beneficial. Ambiguity enters when reality is applied to the model; for example, one may appear to be empowered by their productive efforts while simultaneously unaware of their own state of well-being; even though the earlier premise suggests well-being supports productivity there are likely meaningful interactions within and between the goal areas.

The alignments, linearity, and overall pattern used to structure the Perception Coaching® model and this book are a map created for conceptual

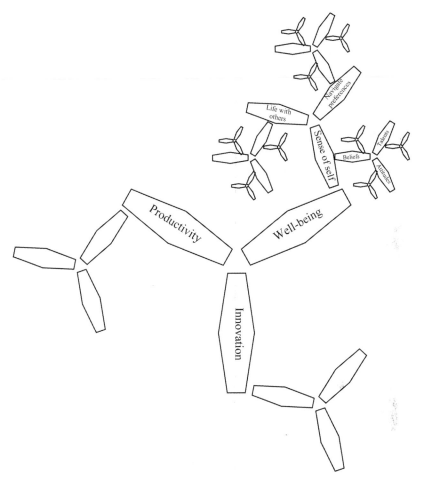

Figure 3.2 The three-branch fractal model is used to begin to map the topics in Parts 2 and 3 of this book. Well-being, productivity, and innovation are simultaneously connected and stand alone as focus areas. Illustration by the author.

convenience which can withstand light scrutiny. Because preferences and experiences vary, individuals do not generally develop in a linear or "well-rounded" manner; they likely have expert skill in some areas, while being a novice in others. This reminds us to avoid overgeneralizing talents or needs, to be aware and responsive as you work others so that development is responsive to individual needs. Best results are accomplished when these tools and concepts are used selectively; coaches access, adapt, and apply information with integrity and flexibility to best meet the unique situations and needs of each client.

Reflect and discuss

1. Describe scenarios in which different reasoning types may be applied.
2. In what ways can you support improved reasoning?
3. How does the aware, engage, empower cycle support growth?
4. What questions might you ask to determine an individual's level of understanding?
5. What intermediate steps might you introduce to help clients transition between levels?
6. With client goals in mind, how might you use the levels or a topic map to create a program of development?

Coaching practices

Goals – a first session outline

When people consider coaching, they often consider if they have enough need, or if there will be sufficient benefit to engage with a coach. There is often an accumulation of evidence before someone seeks a coach; this results in an initial meeting which includes a litany of needs, goals, dreams, and challenges. Looking for themes, scope and sequence of goals, and clarity in expectations will support a mutually satisfactory coaching relationship. To create an atmosphere of success, goals must be clearly defined. People are complex and may have multiple goals and work to grow in many directions at once. Follow these steps to support focused and effective coaching sessions. The initial meeting focuses to provide context, insights regarding topics of interest, as well as preferred communication styles. This first session is also your opportunity to check that together you are a good coach–client fit.

Start with the client's story. Do they immediately have a specific goal in mind? Common broad themes include communication, leadership, productivity, relationship building, and well-being. Value their insight and ask questions for elaboration to clarify the intent of the goal.

Create an inventory or list area in your notes to capture relevant needs, challenges, or opportunities as the client shares their story.

Often clients have a litany of needs, as mentioned earlier. In this case take copious notes or otherwise capture their stories of challenge, success, and hope.

Review the list as a means to share what you heard, as a fact-check with the client before making your coaching response. Ask if they have anything to add or clarify.

When they declare "that is it!" or otherwise indicate they have shared what they intended, it is time to share your expertise. *Consider the list and share themes you notice; this is a form of coaching response.* Ask questions to get their feedback on the themes you sense.

Next steps or next visits

If there remains an undefined need, or the diversity of need defies themes, look for clarity and perspective. Often assessments, brainstorming, and other resources may provide insights to determine potential goals to pursue during the coaching engagement.

If multiple goals emerge, develop a list or card sort activity for the client. They will sort the items into relevant categories such as *Priority (very important)*, *Life-changing (impactful)*, and *Life-enhancing (important)*. To add focus, suggest no more than three very important goals. If there are more than three, prompt them to look for related goals.

If one sorts "improve well-being" into very important and then considers the item "go to the gym," it may help to group using relationships and think of going to the gym as a subgoal or step to improving well-being. Some items sorted into the "lesser" categories may also be related and utilized as steps or subgoals. Other items may provide opportunities for easy wins, as a "test of concept" for strategies, or otherwise be pursued concurrently. This works especially well when the secondary goals are life enhancing, perhaps exercising talents which energizes or supports feeling fulfilled.

Time spent finding the right goal ensures that both client and coaching efforts are beneficial.

Topics and development models

As you likely surmised, Perception Coaching® benefits from a foundation of cognitive psychology integrated with learning and development theories to create flexible approaches for supporting diverse clients and their goals. Specific theoretical underpinnings inform this practice; here they are organized in a meaningful manner to increase the likelihood they are accessible and can be used authentically. Following is a brief outline of the Perception Coaching® landscape complementing the map for Part 2 of this book, designed to support your navigation as you explore goal topics and the strategies and tools with potential to support specific client efforts.

Diverse goals benefit from different developmental models. Perception Coaching® aligns primary topic areas with the following related theoretical approaches. These are supported by goal and effort statements to guide your coaching practice, the clarity of which improves the results of clients' goal and development efforts. Well-being, productivity, and innovation are impact areas which include topics where tensions may exist or there is capacity for growth; in Part 2 these are outlined with related coaching and development strategies. As with other aspects of the Perception Coaching® model, these are convenient pairings; you will likely find value applying development strategies to multiple topics areas to better support specific client needs.

When first meeting clients, they likely come to you with a focus in mind. Though working through each topic in the order below may shine light on unforeseen needs, clarifying topics relevant to their world is essential to meet your clients' needs. Become familiar with the goals and efforts of each topic to be responsive to individuals and their efforts.

Well-being and social-emotional development

Perception Coaching® starts with preferences, naturally developed approaches to understanding and navigating the world around us. Identifying how we naturally do things and the circumstances in which our preferences work provides a foundation from which to grow.

One may enjoy solitude and find themselves often to be the center of attention when in meetings. When preferences are investigated, it turns out that developing expertise is a passion which others appreciate, and sharing expertise feels "life giving" in social situations. Alternatively, when social situations are informal, this same individual discovers that finding appropriate content is difficult and exhausting. Understanding how preferences interact, which give energy, and the efforts required are explored in this section.

Social-emotional development addresses factors which contribute to decisions and resilience, as well as interpersonal dynamics. Development focused on preferences includes exploring talents and attitudes to support effective and sustainable growth to help clients understand others, and to bolster client efforts to address needs for improved well-being.

Productivity and cognitive-behavioral development

Discussion continues to center around our natural way of doing things, and extends to how they may be over-used, create barriers, or lead to gaps in functionality. When focusing on productivity, recognizing preferences and *managing talents* support individuals to make progress.

A person may persuade their children to do chores using star charts, with an extra reward for the child with the most stars. This is implemented at home in a way which shows caring and respect; it is a way to help children learn responsibility and succeed. That same person may publicly display performance data of direct reports as an effort to similarly increase production. Some staff become disengaged, feeling it is a way to demean, threaten, and coerce; perceptual filters also provide insights to how others perceive support for productivity.

Cognitive-behavioral development focuses attention on preferences and strategies to create the best means to support productivity with well-being in mind. Coaching conversations focus on developing supports for progress, strategies to overcome barriers, and skills to produce quality results.

Innovation and opportunity-hypotheses development

Inquiry and creativity are the focus of the third section of Part 2. Combining diverse perspectives, knowledge, and experience leads to creative solutions to demands in the areas of well-being or productivity.

DEI (diversity, equity, and inclusion) is an area of opportunity which many organizations and businesses are embracing. The systemic change required to support diverse cultures, abilities, needs, and expectations requires innovative thinking by individuals, organizations, and societies.

Opportunity is a productive approach to barriers, need fulfillment, and reframing problems. Clients who pursue tough challenges have a purpose which serves to motivate, energize, and inspire their unique solutions.

Efforts focused on the focal development areas are implemented using the Perception Coaching® development framework based on incremental growth from awareness, to engagement, and then empowerment. Working together the Perception Coaching® models and framework provide a map to plan coaching sessions and monitor progress.

Reflect and discuss

1. How are the topics of well-being, productivity, and innovation related?
2. How may understanding the developmental approaches support client growth?
3. How may leadership relate to each of the topics?

4. What focus areas are missing or may exist as a fourth and fifth "main" topic?
5. Thinking about Fred's worry introduced at the beginning of Part 1; imagine Fred's worry is that of a new client:

   a. What aspect of Fred's worry do you want to address?
   b. What developmental approach may align best?
   c. What might you ask Fred? Why?

Coaching with well-being in mind

DOI: 10.4324/9781003332770-5

The broad topics in this section are inclusive of most client goals regarding happiness and comfort. Whether addressing leadership development, team development, entrepreneurship, or specific industry or organizational needs, focusing on well-being supports expectations and provides targeted goal areas which impact client performance.

Well-being

This section takes stock of how we see and experience the world, what we have and need to thrive, and the implications of our values and beliefs. Our natural ways of doing things have developed over time because they work for us. Understand talent-based perceptual filters to see how one can generalize, categorize, and apply useful strategies. Talents help lay bare response patterns so that understanding and evaluation can be explored. Seeing talents clearly provides the first way to develop our perceptions by focusing our attention differently (remember, attention is the key to *sensing*). Focus on awareness moves perceptions and thinking from *implicit to explicit*, a key concept in Perception Coaching®.

Social-emotional development

Social-emotional development shines a light on preferences, how one views and navigates the world, and how preferences guide decisions and interactions with the world. Inspired coaching considers measures of well-being alongside preferences to inform development of emotional intelligence skills and strategies, including sense of self, social functioning, and performance. Shining a light on natural preferences and clarifying the purpose they fulfill is key to supporting clients' ability to perceive more and better navigate life and their environment. When preferences are intentionally used, they support stress management, learning, decision-making, interpersonal communication, and striving for thriving.

As you explore Part 2, keep your coach perspective in mind; recognize both the potential and limitations of the well-being areas outlined. The areas are comprehensive for Perception Coaching®, while leaving space for connections and other goals. Consider areas you prefer, in which you have or desire to develop expertise; perhaps there is a goal topic which does not seem to be addressed. These may indicate a niche area for you as a coach. Make the content your own by continuing to add these and your own relevant questions and strategies to your toolbox.

Self-concept
and well-being

4

Goal: Healthy life and outlook; authentic self is thriving.

Efforts: Social-emotional development and managing relevant areas of wellness and health with preferences in mind.

Understanding well-being and how to improve it may describe the most relevant and ambiguous goals faced by clients. This is because feelings related to well-being are the result of ongoing interactions between attitudes and environments. Coaching is called upon to support goals focused on quality of life, personal development, and navigating career or social situations. Each area of life deemed relevant can, at any given time, be considered to have its own state of well-being; the state of well-being in one aspect of life will influence the others.

In *A Theory of Human Motivation*, Abraham Maslow put forth his hierarchy of needs (1943). This model provides a touchpoint to understand and support human behavior, needs, and development which is especially useful because it is familiar to practitioners in numerous industries and social sciences. Theoretically, the pyramid model for Maslow's hierarchy indicates that lower needs must be satisfied before those higher may be addressed, the ultimate goal being self-actualization. Often daily efforts are performed solely to meet basic and psychological needs (the lowest and second tiers of the pyramid, respectively). Maslow noted that not everyone reaches self-actualization, or their full potential, perhaps because many people spend their day working to meet their basic needs. Coaching goals which consider safety, comfort, and purpose related to self-actualization with an individual's preferences in mind

DOI: 10.4324/9781003332770-6

support well-being. Consideration is also given to meeting these needs when building capacity in teams and organizations, serving as a practical reminder that members have diverse needs and preferences.

Whether client visits include an individual, team, or organization, Perception Coaching® supports an attitude and culture of learning and innovation, recognizing both needs and accomplishments, addressing challenges, and supporting development. Coaching starts with understanding self before exploring how to better understand others, because access to sense of self through experiences and reflection builds a foundation from which to begin sensing preferences of others. When we understand how our preferences influence our perceptions, we are better able to question how we see others. Not only that, when engaging in change and development, the person anyone can control most effectively is themselves. For goals focused on thinking of others and relationships see the Navigate Life with Others section, though developing one's sense of self is the best first step to understanding others.

Coaching provides a means to support the efforts of others to go beyond merely meeting their needs to be their best selves. Coaches help individuals to develop intention and perceptions to shift from naturally supporting safety to sensing opportunities for thriving and flourishing. Imagine a world where self-actualization is in everyone's reach. This requires focus, for which coaching is key. To paraphrase Voltaire, *no problem can withstand the assault of sustained* **attention**. The role of the coach is to keep goals in focus, front of mind, and moving forward to support the efforts of clients as they strive for their highest potential.

Whatever a client's preferences and current state, their well-being benefits from increased awareness and understanding of the factors involved. Improved well-being helps individuals to thrive and their potential to flourish.

Impactful factors

Well-being awareness includes understanding our preferences and how they contribute to our sense of safety, comfort, and success. Everyone has a unique profile of preferences which influence what they see, feel, and think. As mentioned in the section regarding perceptions, this influence tends to be self-reinforcing. Perceptions filter for efficiency; the by-product of this streamlining is less thinking, for better or worse! As we explore well-being, implications of self-concept, navigating the world, and interacting with others are considered and coaching is focused on social-emotional development to bring understanding from aware to empowered.

Clients' sense of well-being includes different aspects of their needs and life. Factors which interact with well-being include preferences, safety, and social and emotional skills; these are explored through sense of self, working to thrive and grow authentically, and attitudes and understanding.

Self-actualization is the peak of the hierarchy for our immediate purpose, though circa 1969 Maslow included a higher level titled *self-transcendence* (see Koltko-Rivera, 2006). This suggests a continuum from basic to mature regarding the ability to shift focus from self to something greater. Individuals begin life primarily concerned with self and their own needs. However, most people know individuals for whom self seems to rarely be the focus, often caregivers or parents; their focus is on the needs of others when considering decisions, values, and priorities. Perception Coaching® views *me*, *we*, and *they* thoughts as equally appropriate and valued, not as a continuum of development but where context and needs provide significant indicators for whose perspectives are considered in thinking.

Sense of self and direction

This section outlines the relevance of sense of self, activities to identify preferences, as well as the benefits and barriers sense of self can create.

Self-concept reflects feelings of competence and self-esteem connected to accomplishment. Realistic self-concept is not overinflated by success, nor undermined by failure; it includes holistic evaluation of talents, needs, and growth opportunities. When accompanied by an attitude of productive resilience, it is referred to as self-accepting. Self-rejecting describes the perspective of someone who defines themselves by their failures, and feels they hold little value. These attitudes affect mood and often one's overall sense of well-being. The greatest contributor to pride and self-concept is to succeed where both effort and skill are challenged. The primary function of excuses and rationalizations is to protect one's sense of self. These last two points are important to keep in mind when considering progress on development activities and making risk assessments.

Individuals' sense of self is influenced by others, positively and negatively, which can support or undermine having realistic self-concepts. Mirror theory posits that self-concept develops as a result of others' evaluation of competence. Accurately sensing approval and reproach, as well as understanding the intentions and preferences of others, should be explored when one's sense of self appears to be developed primarily or excessively through feedback from others.

For Perception Coaching®, sense of self begins with an increasing aware-ness of preferences and competencies focused on beliefs, talents, and atti-tudes. As awareness of a preference grows, the preference is available for reflection and evaluation.

Beliefs and cognitive dissonance

Tensions are often the result of conflicts which likely include unidentified beliefs or other implicitly developed dispositions. Cognitive dissonance cre-ates an undercurrent of unease, and it is not always clear what cognitions are at odds. Exploring beliefs supports clarity for overcoming these tensions.

Beliefs

Beliefs guide attention, thoughts, behaviors, and interactions. The context in which beliefs are discussed here is not spiritual or religious. Beliefs are core preferences, developed as implicit cognitive responses in early childhood. They are foundational to sense of self and deserve thoughtful consideration. Beliefs are formed automatically in response to environmental stimuli, pri-marily before abstract or complex thinking skills are developed. Therefore, when focused on beliefs, perceptive coaching conversations begin by explor-ing awareness.

Coaches appreciate the relevance of clients' beliefs while recognizing that strong beliefs are preferential opinions which have been implicitly reinforced and developed. Beliefs are truths individuals hold, though they cannot be sub-stantiated. The idea behind the belief is charged with both logic and wishful thinking; the belief makes sense, rings true, feels right, or is validated by a *gut check*. Once a belief is established, related information about the belief is selectively explored; reinforcing evidence and correlations are inferred, lend-ing credibility to the truth of the belief. Contrary evidence goes unnoticed or is likely discounted as an exception.

Beliefs act as a navigation tool, supporting thoughts and actions as we navi-gate life. Imagine implications for the belief: *people who are late are disrespectful*. A person holding that belief likely lives a pattern of punctuality, accompa-nied by frustration when faced with those for whom punctuality is a struggle. Their belief is internally reinforced when someone arrives late and their auto-matic thought is something like, *I respect your time, so I arrived a little early*. The inherent assumption, people who are late don't respect the time of others, feels true and makes sense when the behaviors of others are seen through their own motivations. This reinforcing information is collected every time someone is early, on time, or late, making the belief robust.

Beliefs may include logical fallacy or thought errors – the belief that late behavior is explained by a lack of respect is oversimplistic. Many people had great success being on time during the pandemic, when meetings were almost exclusively online. Travel, meeting space, food, and other everyday worries and tasks were greatly reduced, making punctuality easier to accomplish for more people more often; it is unlikely this increased timeliness is an indication of changes in respect levels. Returning to in-person meetings has, for some, created a need to re-learn the scheduling and planning strategies they practiced regularly before the great interruption to in-person meetings caused by the pandemic. When isolation was reduced, early face-to-face meetings included participant talk about forgetting how to plan and navigate commutes, while some people were still hesitant to meet with others. These issues and needs resulted in more people being late, a change that, once again, has not been directly correlated to respect.

Beliefs are robust; an idea that was formative for the belief can be found to be in error and the belief will continue to be held. Consider the belief *people who are late are disrespectful*: the above narrative may be followed by evidence that contradicts a positive correlation between timeliness and respect. Perhaps a student was late to class, the teacher felt disrespected. Later the teacher found that the student had to leave work precisely on time and catch two buses to attend the class; it was surprising that they were not late more often. The student had heard great things about the teacher and went out of their way to be there because of the respect they had for that teacher. Because beliefs are strong, counterexamples are often thought of as *the exception that makes the rule*. Filipowicz et al. (2018) in their study of mental models found that observed changes, even surprising ones, do not result in updating beliefs. Participants in the study often viewed the change information as outliers and dismissed the change evidence.

Beliefs can be reinforced by information that should undermine them; this may be considered a defining quality of beliefs. Reinforcement in the face of contradiction is counterintuitive, yet a possible result when cognitive dissonance is experienced.

Cognitive dissonance

Beliefs, values, and attitudes are *cognitions* or implicit responses to environmental information and experiences. Most beliefs form in early childhood before abstract thought is developed and the beliefs operate without one being aware of their influence. It is generally assumed that people naturally align their beliefs, values, attitudes, and behaviors as they develop, because these traits are instrumental for us to operate and understand other people. In a summary, McGuire described the last section as being "devoted to second thoughts regarding whether the person's belief system is really as highly interconnected and as internally consistent as I chose to assume" (1968, p. 142). McGuire's expertise included theories for mapping the structure of human thought and he was an influential researcher for decades in the psychology of persuasion. His assumption was individuals have belief systems which are consistent to support our understanding of ourselves and the world. For convenience, and logically, we assume our underlying cognitive systems make sense. What happens when they do not?

Perception and subsequent learning, as we discussed earlier, affords one many opportunities for interpretation. This is done without an explicit, rational, logical process, which potentially results in ambiguous cognitions. Cognitive dissonance occurs when inconsistent cognitions are held. Beliefs and ideas resulting in contradictions are often visible in the tensions and barriers faced by clients. When a belief or set of beliefs developed in childhood is in opposition to developed behaviors, sense of self, or goals, stress thresholds drop and there is tension. Levy et al. (2018) found when faced with incongruent endings to simple prompts participants had negative affective responses across self-reports, last word physiological responses using electromyographic and electroencephalographic measures, and implicit ratings. When faced with dissonance, there is motivation to resolve perceived inconsistency through sense-making; this is regularly done implicitly, though the resulting tensions may become explicitly visible.

In essence, beliefs are operationalized opinions that may be changed. This is no simple feat. Aronson (1968) describes Leon Festinger's famous example of rationalizations used to overcome inconsistent cognitions. In Leon Festinger's example the source of cognitive dissonance is a cigarette smoker's belief that cigarette smoking causes cancer. We assume that the smoker would like to avoid cancer; their smoking behavior and belief it is risky provide the psychological inconsistency. The natural conclusion is they should stop smoking. It is not easy to overcome a smoking habit, hence these possible rationalizations: dismiss the inevitability of cancer by reasoning that most data are clinical not experimental (no control groups), I smoke filtered which are safer, other people do it so it cannot be that bad, I really like it so it is worth the risk, or I am a rebel and like living on the edge. Cigarette smoking seems reckless in the long term, and we can see how a smoker might grapple with this tension. The rationalization, though not logical, effectively relieves cognitive dissonance. Many sources of cognitive dissonance are more difficult to detect and relieve.

Beliefs are planted in early childhood by observing the environment; children notice people interacting in certain ways and are bombarded with messages from media and immediate contacts. The reinforced thoughts and behaviors indicate important ideas and beliefs develop. Common themes are seen in advice, idioms, and stories children hear and they trigger emotions which give energy to beliefs. Consider how many of the following phrase sets include familiar messages. Try harder, hard work pays off, be an ant not a grasshopper. Early risers are successful, an early start gives you time to make your day great, the early bird catches the worm. Focus, if you stick with it you will succeed, be the tortoise not the hare. Be nice, if you are nice to others, they will be nice to you, practice the golden rule. Competition makes us stronger, be a winner, may the best (man) win. Reinforcing ideas are often intentional and can create strong beliefs. Cultural and societal norms are reflected in beliefs, and though they may shift, many beliefs have been reinforced for generations.

Another source of belief formation is knowledge or information gaps. Golman and Loewenstein (2018) explore a theory to predict when people will obtain or avoid information and when they will seek or avoid ambiguity and risk. Here also, emotions play a role in belief development by directing attention through the discomfort of uncertainty. On first thought, beliefs explain something in a way that is attributed to common sense or things everyone knows. Yet there are implications and possible contradictions when ideas are generalized and set as a belief rather than a guideline. When beliefs are established, we are generally unaware of them, and the resulting answers, benefits, and tensions they create as we navigate the day-to-day world are inexplicable.

If someone simultaneously holds the beliefs that *it is important to be nice* and *winners will succeed*, tension may grow when winning creates losers; a win may simultaneously feel like an accomplishment and an unkindness to others. If they have trouble sleeping and simultaneously hold an operational belief that early risers are successful, frustration will occur as sleep deprivation sets in due to the desire to wake early. In either case, cognitive dissonance may not be apparent, though they likely feel the effects of the tension created by their beliefs.

Because beliefs are formed early, before individuals are experienced with abstract thought, they develop without abstract reasoning. This leads to the potential of holding contradicting beliefs or misalignment with other preferences and behaviors. The belief itself acts as an invisible source of stress and confusion because the mind treats it as accepted fact existing in dissonance with coexisting yet opposing beliefs, capacities, and adopted values. Self-sabotage may also indicate cognitive dissonance. There are abundant stories of gifted students becoming underachievers who sacrifice their success to help others, who avoid surpassing those they care about, and who begin to fail to avoid attention; awareness of related beliefs provides insight so learners may better navigate achievement.

Resolution of cognitive dissonance happens in many ways, some mentioned in Leon Festinger's example. There are both primitive and evolved means for facing belief dilemmas, mostly dependent on the level of awareness and engagement with the beliefs in question. In Abelson et al., their proposed framework includes three types of resolution: cognitive, perceptual, and behavioral, which are dependent on motivation, prior learning, personality, and the context which exacerbates the tension (1968, p. 656).

Overt consideration of beliefs and possible dissonance is an important approach to challenge and tension when using Perception Coaching®. By calling upon rational processes to evaluate the affective function of beliefs, core beliefs can be openly developed and adopted rather than operating on beliefs by default. Effective starting points are often indicated in industry- or role-based literature.

For instance, leaders in senior level positions often hold beliefs that they may credit for success, but which may also contribute to reduced well-being. The topic of sleep and established beliefs is of interest in this demographic because many leaders work long hours and feel sleep deprived. In a previous paragraph this series of messages was shared: early risers are successful, an early start gives you time to make your day great, the early bird catches the worm. Whether beliefs related to these sentiments are held true or not, they are socially powerful. Svetieva et al. (2017) studied sleep, performance, and related beliefs of senior level leaders and discovered misguided beliefs which likely contribute to poor sleep patterns. They found that one of the biggest predictors of sleep problems was an inability to psychologically detach from work. On the positive side, their results also indicate that exercise benefits better sleep. Guiding exploration regarding an executive's specific beliefs about sleep, productivity, and success clarifies expectations, uncovers opportunities to create boundaries, and may provide motivation to revise beliefs. Constructively navigating cognitive dissonance is possible. When coaching, start building awareness of beliefs with an eye to the future.

Reflect and discuss

1. When is it useful to explore beliefs related to time?
2. How might exploring their own beliefs challenge a client?
3. What support might you offer a client struggling with cognitive dissonance?

Coaching practices

Tensions and barriers – discover implicitly drawn conclusions

Start with awareness. *What core beliefs help you navigate everyday life?*

Aware: The implicit nature of beliefs means they may be ill-defined or undiscovered
Warm up: *What are your favorite sayings, quotes, or idioms?*
Main question: *What core beliefs help you navigate everyday life?*

Engaged: Beliefs work in the background often unnoticed
How have your beliefs contributed to success or happiness?
How may your beliefs get in the way of your success or well-being?

Empowered: Beliefs provide direction and hope
What limiting beliefs do you hold? (They may be the ones getting in the way, described above.)
What overt attention or action can help you begin to explore the belief and its implications?

Note: Engaged and empowered level questions may be "homework" to process more deeply between coaching sessions.

Sustainable strategies are those found by exploring what clients naturally do and think. At an early age people exhibit characteristic dispositions, approaches, interests, and ways of acting and thinking. Beliefs are borne of childhood. Another aspect of the natural ways of doing, thinking, and relating is talent; whether raw or examined and developed, natural talents contribute significantly to sense of self.

Talents and development

Talents are natural approaches and responses to stimuli which tend to produce reinforcing results. When someone's *way of doing* is noticed, consider how the thinking or behavior may have developed; how it may meet the needs of the person. Coaching that starts with talents is meaningful because it reinforces the client's power while providing valuable perspective on ways to succeed, needs, and perhaps limitations. When a client can recognize things that others may do better, this opens them up to focus their efforts on using their own talents and support others to use their talents. Investments made in what one naturally does well provide the highest return on development efforts; opportunities to grow are bolstered by intentional practice and stretching of these innate abilities.

Talents

Everyone has talents, natural patterns of approaches, dispositions, and behaviors used to understand and navigate the world. Talents appear in the ways we think, behave, and interact with others, ideas, and things. Talents demonstrate preferences which influence how we sense and understand the world. The perspective that talents have great potential power, as well as potential to interfere with success, fuels talent-based development. Areas impacted by both recognized and unidentified talents include well-being, relationships, productivity, leadership, innovation, and communication.

When talents are overused or used in an inappropriate context, they are weaknesses; this can be the result of a talent which is unexamined. Perceived weaknesses are not ignored in talent-based development; to mitigate weakness, identify the related talent and explore more productive applications of the talent, or access another talent in that situation. Coaching supports clients to manage needs and challenges through development of talents and implementation of systems to mitigate tensions and deficiencies. When talents are developed and mature, they are less likely to show up as weaknesses.

Talents are exceptional by nature; they appear and develop unevenly. An individual who is comfortable, even captivating, as a speaker discussing their most recent adventure in a seminar may not be equally effective facilitating a group planning an adventure. As a speaker, they may have a larger-than-life presence in the room, craft a story in a manner which engages the audience, and naturally keep the attention of all. As a facilitator, some of those talents may interfere with participants' attention to tasks or each other while doing group work. The speaker may not have the talents that support responding to individual needs which are essential for quality facilitation. The approaches, strategies, and skills for presenting and facilitating may or may not be transferrable, depending on the speaker's talents.

Some individuals seem to have unlimited talent which they apply effectively and seem to be able to do anything! Perhaps this is evidence of a strong talent or an intuitive use of multiple talents. There is no comprehensive list of talents or preferences; talents are diverse traits which vary in intensity, application, and appearance. What holds true is that talents are noteworthy; they include preferred ways of thinking, relating, and behaving which are useful for navigating the world. Identifying talents supports realistic self-concept and contributes to developing sense of self. Identifying talents can be accomplished anecdotally and via a variety of assessments.

First, explore and analyze success, achievement, and accomplishment as means to identify talents. What is your most recent accomplishment? Responses such as X was easy, I was in the zone, I could not stop working on Y, or I always enjoy Z all indicate talent is at work. When exploring success, take time to discover the circumstances that created the ease or flow and dive deeper into identifying and understanding the natural inclination that was triggered.

Second, through observation and questioning notice patterns of behaviors as well as ways of relating and thinking which indicate talents. Generally ask, *What is something you always Do?* Explore talents relevant to current goals using more specific questions. *How do you do projects? What is the source of most of your projects? Where do you start? Do you have routines of thinking or doing? How do you usually interact with others?*

Affectively negative responses may indicate talent, too. When asked, "What do you do when faced with a challenge?" a client may respond, "I avoid challenges." This declaration seems like an endpoint; it is a bold statement which indicates the likelihood of a richer response behind it. Follow up with, "What do you mean?" You may find that avoiding challenge indicates a strategic mind at work, a person who is content with their current reality, or yet other possibilities. Pursue responses with follow-up questions to discover talents, needs, and opportunities for exploration.

When asked about collaboration, a client responded, "I interrupt too much, and I can't help it." Chronic behaviors often indicate needs and talents. Not only that, but their stated judgment is a disempowering belief which undermines both client efforts and the support a coach may offer. One means to address this is to understand the behavior by becoming curious about the talents which support it.

Third, assessments provide a unique opportunity to identify talents and preferences. Loosely categorized as psychological or personality tests, most talent assessments differ in their theoretical underpinnings and provide alternative perspectives on traits and how one operates in the world. In addition to being valued for unique perspectives, assessments can be used to clarify and establish language useful for expressing and understanding the ill-defined ideas of character traits and soft skills.

When talents are made visible and developed, opportunities for the individual to shine increase, and talent becomes strength. Developing one's talents is a lifelong journey of growth.

Development

Focusing goals on preferences acknowledges what is wonderfully unique about an individual and encourages their natural tendencies to serve them well. Contrast this with the effort required to achieve goals focused on deficiency or weakness. Doing something you do well so that you can do it even better is naturally reinforcing and enjoyable. Working on something that you don't prefer and which has been frustrating in the past so that you can do more of it is a challenge even the most determined among us likely avoid.

Developing talent is easier than fixing deficits. Talents and preferences contribute to the uniqueness of a person; developing their natural traits supports an individual to be their best self! To develop talent, we must appreciate, grow, and encourage diverse expressions of talent. Experiences, events, and world view vary by individual; these create both similarities and differences among people. How we perceive these similarities and differences impacts how we navigate change, diversity, and relationships.

Pronounced differences provide opportunities for perspectives which should not be dismissed; differences should be explored and valued to increase our understanding of the world around us. Developing natural talents is the most effective way to create beneficial skills and strategies, and it happens while recognizing and appreciating a unique part of the individual. The apparent specialization in areas of talent does not limit roles or career opportunities but provides the best ways to succeed in many endeavors. If talent is a spotlight shining on success, development is the means to broaden its scope. Talent development focuses on intentionally doing more of what you do well, supporting your natural ways of doing while experience contributes to expertise; the intentional interaction between preferences and expertise is then aimed at creating predictable success.

Reflect and discuss

Consider how beliefs and talents contribute to sense of self.

1. What helps one to see strengths?
2. What supports understanding needs?

3. How do you identify and mitigate weaknesses?
4. How might exploring their own talents challenge a client?
5. What support might you offer a client struggling with talent development?

Coaching practices

Focus growth – increase the range of natural light

Aware: Talents work in the background, often unnoticed
Warm up: *What are your favorite activities, events, or interests?*
Main question: *What talents help you navigate everyday life?*

Engaged: Start by engaging natural talents
How have your talents contributed to success or happiness?
How may your talents get in the way of your success or well-being?

Empowered: Talents and self-concept are a source of hope
What talents do you take for granted? (These are hidden contributors to success.)
What overt attention or action can help you begin to see them and use them more often?

Note: Engaged and empowered level questions may be "homework" to process more deeply between coaching sessions.

Developing talents is an endeavor which is both engaging and rewarding. Understanding one's talents builds a strong sense of self and opens one's senses to the talents of others.

Attitudes and positive psychology

Attitudes are an enduring judgment based on the generalized feelings about things, emerging when experiences, beliefs, and preferences interact. Attitudes can be positive, negative, or apathetic, depending on perceptions related to the interactions. Positive attitudes contribute to well-being and optimism.

Attitude

People can find puzzles irresistible. Some see connections all around. Some enjoy telling or hearing stories. Some see beauty in patterns. Some see perfection in diversity. Each preference we have supports an attitude of appreciation, and the opposite is true; we often have dislikes that appear as attitudes. These preferences influence how we see related features in the environment; attitudes implicitly support perceptions, decisions, and direction. Attitudes are often expressed in one's assumptions, approaches, perspectives, or mindsets. *I love math* and *I am terrible at math* are statements that indicate different attitudes toward math. Both perspectives may have started with a classroom experience, grades in school, balancing a checkbook, or other factors; over time reinforcing experiences and emotions evolve the sentiment into an overgeneralized mindset. Strong attitudes are charged with emotion; when held as absolute, they become a barrier to seeing other perspectives.

Unexplained perceived variability in an attitude can interfere with one's sense of self. One may enjoy learning, be deeply engaged in the process of learning, and have great focus when mastering content; the same individual may find that being told how to do something is unenjoyable. When inner conflict is detected, confidence is undermined; this is mitigated through reflection and reasoning. As attitudes are analyzed and understood, like beliefs, they can be adapted or abandoned if they are not productive.

When more is understood about the differences in contradicting attitudes, the implicit is made explicit and sense of self matures. Coaching conversations about attitudes often result in discussion about the generalizable aspects of values and talents, and the unique qualities related to the attitude that are seen as apparent contradictions.

For instance, one may strive for consistency and simultaneously resist creating daily habits. A coach hypothesizes to understand an individual whose attitude toward consistency is appreciation, yet they struggle with creating productive habits. Perhaps they are reluctant to add routines to their many existing responsibilities because they will not be able to consistently perform them.

Alternatively, they may perceive their own consistency differently than the consistency of others. Consistent behaviors may feel restrictive; having freedom to change course or take risks is preferred. Yet, consistent behaviors in others leads to predictability, which is preferred to build trust.

Hypotheses are valuable, providing a place to consider possibilities, questions, and evidence from stories. The client has their truth, and the coach's role is to provide space and prompts which support the client to explore it. Once analyzed, contextual information can clarify apparent internal contradictions. Analysis and reflection have the potential to develop sense of self, as well as an understanding of how the concept interacts with perceptions.

Bias box

Tensions

Finding opportunity in the presence of problems is the most productive means to overcome significant or chronic tensions.

Chronic problems take up a lot of space in one's mind and life. Addressing especially sticky tensions leads one to be immersed in negativity, in problematic causes and consequences. When no clear means to make progress are visible, one becomes demoralized and fatigued. Efforts spent exploring a challenge to understand it leave little energy or space for creating solutions; standard solutions do not address the complexity or persistence of such challenges. Navigate past understanding challenges and decisions to actively evaluate, adopt, and shift attitudes and perceptions to improve strategies and respond productively. Goals present a positive counterpoint to tensions; they shift attention away from the negativity of the problem to focus on making progress.

Challenge: When a barrier is present, identify it. A barrier exists when there is no visible way to address it; a path must be created or discovered to circumvent or mitigate problems.

Often when progress stagnates or stops completely frustration sets in. One may think *Why can't I do this? Why does this always happen?* This is the moment to recognize the challenge. Recognize the pain point or circumstance when the challenge is present. Ask: What is getting in the way? When does this issue occur?

Opportunity: Shift focus from removing the persistent challenge to sensing a better future. What does life look like without the challenge? From that vision of a better life, one works to see opportunities from which that better future can be created.

Coaching to envision an optimistic future provides both hope and focus. Time, energy, and efforts are directed with the end in mind. The direction is set, coaching conversations focus on experiences and strategies which make progress toward the goals.

Goals: Working toward goals which build a better future is empowering and productive and likely overwhelming. Identify and pursue optimistic goals to pursue the vision. Consider developing a system which would mitigate the problem, actions to prevent future issues, etc.

Goal setting questions should align with preferences. Whether small tasks are preferred (What is a small, easy step?) or projects with big results (What would make the biggest impact?) or a combination of goals, to support success consider how talents will contribute to goal attainment.

Self-assess

Which step in navigating challenges is easiest for you to address? For each pair mark the strength of your preference between the two anchors; the center is neutral, indicating no preference.

Challenge ---- 3 ---- 2 ---- 1 ---- 0 ---- 1 ---- 2 ---- 3 ---- Opportunity
Challenge ---- 3 ---- 2 ---- 1 ---- 0 ---- 1 ---- 2 ---- 3 ---- Goals
Goals ---- 3 ---- 2 ---- 1 ---- 0 ---- 1 ---- 2 ---- 3 ---- Opportunity

Note the order and strength of your preferences.

Reflect and discuss

Consider the purpose, values, and benefits of the three steps:

1. Describe circumstance or content for which tensions may exist in:

    - identification and understanding root causes
    - reframing a challenge as an opportunity
    - goal setting.

2. The potential impact of facing challenges is great. How do you support the shift from "admiring the problem" to seeing an optimistic future?
3. How does this contribute to your coaching perspective?

Positive psychology

Historically, psychology was predominantly focused on fixing or mediating disorders and perceived dysfunction. Martin Seligman, often credited with founding positive psychology, explored happiness as the focus of psychological study and offered the PERMA model to understand aspects of flourishing, the factors of which are positive emotions, engagement, relationships, meaning, and achievement (visit www.authenichappiness.org to learn more). Also related, Self-Determination Theory by Edward L. Deci and Richard M. Ryan first requires one's needs for competence, connection, and autonomy be satisfied for flourishing. The RAW model for flourishing (Green & Palmer, 2019) provides yet another perspective on what is important, including resilience, achievement, and well-being. All indicate the productive impact positive emotions have on human capacity, providing sufficient foundations to recommend positive psychology as a lever for effective coaching.

Optimal functioning is the goal of positive psychology; related topics include mindfulness, optimism, strengths, and positive emotions. Of psychological approaches, positive psychology is used by 57% of coaches and 69% of coaching psychologists (Palmer & Whybrow, 2017). Though definitions of positive psychology may vary, the idea that positive approaches are beneficial for development appears to have consensus.

Furthermore, processing negative messages is cognitively more difficult than positive messages. Indeed, Agmon et al. (2022), Bremnes et al. (2022), Huang et al. (2022), and Rück et al. (2021) among numerous others have experimented with a variety of factors, including different language and visual cues, and continue to add credibility to the polarity interaction. Verifying the truth of negative sentences requires more cognitive energy than those without a negative, because extra effort is required to reverse the truth of the integral affirmation. The negative itself lacks meaning; only when the positive is understood can one make sense of the negative. This extra cognitive load has the potential to increase misconceptions. The previous statement is not untrue. Hearing or reading statements with a double negative can leave one second-guessing their interpretation. Therefore, *be positive* may be seen as more than an optimistic approach; it is an approach for which related messages are more efficiently understood.

Sensing opportunities to shine, grow, and appreciate is enhanced by productive attitudes. More good is visible when you have an intentional bias for seeing it. Productive attitudes make space for optimism.

Coaching practices

Increase optimism – prioritize productive attitudes

Explore existing attitudes. *What attitudes help you effectively navigate everyday life?*

Aware: A strong sense of self accounts for preferences including attitudes.
Warm up: *What are your most powerful feelings?*
Main question: *What positive attitudes guide your attention, interests, and goals?*

Engaged: Attitudes are often subject or topic specific.
What are some of your favorite things?
How have your attitudes contributed to success or happiness?
How may your attitude get in the way of your success or well-being?

Empowered: Attitude shifts influence perceptive shifts.
*Does your attitude serve to **protect you** or **give you hope** for the future?*

What attitudes support your well-being, help you relate to others, or help you get things done?
What productive attitudes will you adopt and nurture?

Sample productive attitude phrases:

- Everyone has talents
- Curiosity grows confidence
- Everyone is doing their best
- You are important
- Everyone is both unique and similar
- We have common ground
- You make the world a better place
- Emotional information is important

Note: Engaged and empowered level questions may be "homework" used to process more deeply between coaching sessions.

Sense of self develops as one reflects, explores, and understands more of one's preferences, recognizes how one's preferences impact interactions and decisions, and then navigates the world with realistic self-concepts, learning and growing with preferences in mind.

Confidence grows as preferences are used to intentionally support understanding, decisions, development, and success. Perception Coaching® is beneficial when preferences cause tension or interfere with productive thoughts and actions. Related preferences are explicitly processed and evaluated; this may lead to a preference being reframed or ignored.

Reflect and discuss

1. What are your natural ways of doing things when it comes to understanding yourself?
2. When is it useful to explore negative attitudes?
3. How might exploring their own attitudes challenge a client?
4. What support might you offer a client struggling with optimism?
5. How might you use the concept of cognitive dissonance?
6. How might positive psychology be useful in coaching?
7. Refer to Appendix Table A.1; select a client profile.

   a. What questions might you pose regarding sense of self?
   b. What indicates an opportunity to explore sense of self?

Beliefs, talents, and attitudes are cognitions and preferences which shape the way we sense and interact with the world around us. Developing understanding of these factors supports both sense of self and awareness of our perceptual filters. Well-being is impacted by our awareness of and comfort with our preferences. A strong sense of self supports the ability to respond when preferences are "offended" or not met.

Navigate preferences

Well-being and accomplishment are best supported when the implications of preferences including talents and beliefs are understood. Preferences develop as a guide to navigate the world safely. When preferences are clear, working to increase opportunities to do what one does well is an especially impactful goal. Reflect and explore relationships between preferences and well-being in a variety of environments. Plan and implement strategies to advocate for talents and needs to support quality of life in the moment and over time.

Navigating preferences presupposes awareness of preferences and includes strategies which build *response bridges* when preferences feel ignored or offended. Strategies to understand beliefs, talents, and attitudes also allow us to shift preferences which no longer serve us.

Strategies such as suspending judgment, analyzing beliefs, and adopting productive attitudes are useful to pause the brain's autopilot and recalibrate navigation to support higher goals, rather than focusing on safety. This recalibration is especially powerful when one feels dissatisfied.

Response bridges support one to slow one's immediate reaction to move beyond a negative response to see other perspectives and respond more objectively, and productively. The well-being of all involved is supported when one maintains a calm demeanor.

During the reaction slow down, look for new perspectives using internal questioning and reframing with the goal to seek ways to better align circumstances and your preferences. Internal questioning with the goal to sense potential in the form of purpose or opportunity will create a productive response bridge. Reframe the circumstance by considering positive intentions or outcomes which may result; this reframed perspective may not be your preference yet can still create a response supportive of improved well-being. When a deficit or offense is noticed, focus to effectively communicate expectations or needs related to preferences; this response bridge counters frustration or anger, and will increase a sense of well-being.

Emotional awareness and management

When safety, comfort, or success are threatened or at risk, well-being suffers and will benefit from support. Social-emotional development addresses sense of self and attitudes as means to help one understand feelings and authentically work to thrive and grow, both independently and with others. Coaching conversations exploring these areas seek to provide insights which lead to strategies for improving and maintaining well-being.

Emotions as notifications

Emotions capture and guide our attention, but not only that – they also implicitly and indirectly influence our understanding of the event; this influence results in a positive or negative interpretation. Even if we actively suppress emotional information by ignoring or dismissing feelings and emotions, refusing it attention does not lessen the impact of the emotional information. It implicitly influences related thoughts and behaviors.

Much like talents, emotions can be developed and matured. When emotions are unexplored or raw, their affect may be disproportionate to the circumstances. Mature emotions and emotional responses encourage cognitive processes to engage, producing a measured response. Emotions often indicate a threat, are a call to action, or need reflection to process for meaning; developing effective strategies to navigate feelings and emotions is essential for well-being. Environments in which emotions are managed are not devoid of feeling. In fact, those involved provide space so emotions receive attention appropriate to their purpose; they are sensed and processed so the information they indicate is noticed and analyzed appropriately.

Because of its often-unseen influence, we concentrate on the power emotion has for improving well-being. Emotions (subconscious mind) and feelings (conscious mind) are responses to experiences and sensations. One may feel hungry, which is qualitatively different than the emotions of joy, anger, or sadness. Feelings may be considered an expression of basic needs, revisiting Maslow's hierarchy of needs. Emotion may express the state of basic needs and higher needs; feelings are often viewed as a component of emotion. Mood is also relevant; it is a generalized feeling. A mood may be obvious, though the source of a mood is often hard to determine, even with intentional inquiry. Mood lowers the threshold for triggering related emotions. Positive emotions are elicited more easily when one is in a good mood; when in a bad mood, it is easier to trigger negative emotions.

Managing emotions

Emotions function as both notification and pressure release when preferences or needs are offended or especially well-aligned. Emotions are specific reactions which trigger both physiological and cognitive changes to prepare for action, functioning as an alert system for preferences at work. In the absence of attention, emotions dissipate quickly; when emotional responses are uncomfortable, they may be acted upon or ignored. Dismissing emotions buries important information. To be of use, emotions need to be attended to differently. By considering factors which accompanied the emotion when it was experienced, the source of emotional reaction can be found. The short life of emotion makes pinpointing the root cause or trigger simpler if it is done immediately; over time influencing factors may be forgotten. Individuals can more effectively manage responses by identifying circumstances which evoke strong emotions.

Emotions influence self-concept and self-expression, interactions with others, as well as interactions within the environment. Feelings of safety, comfort, and accomplishment were introduced through the lens of preference. These needs can also be understood by focusing on emotions and emotional intelligence. One can prepare for or ensure their preferred level of each need. Decisions are made daily by weighing options that include some level of risk. If the risk is tolerable, one may compromise safety or comfort to invest effort toward growth or success. Alternatively, when one has exerted effort over time, success may be sacrificed for safety or comfort.

When disasters occur, people are often faced with decisions that put safety, comfort, and accomplishment in stark relief. Emotions influence individuals' decisions to protect their home, move to a safer place, and help others. Life choices similarly include consideration of risk tolerances. Leaving a familiar job for a new role has implications for future safety, comfort, and accomplishment; processing involves comparing feelings about the current situation with the hopes and worries one has for the new opportunity. Energy, values, talents, as well as risk tolerance and other factors give rise to emotions which contribute to selecting one of the innumerable paths available. By attending to emotions and emotional responses, one can ensure that the paths they take feel right and lead in the intended direction.

Reflect and discuss

1. How are preferences and emotions connected?
2. How may managing emotions support client efforts?

3. What indicates a need to refer a client for mental health support?
4. Refer to Appendix Table A.1; select a client profile.

    a. What questions might you pose regarding emotions?
    b. What indicates an opportunity to explore emotions?

Coaching practices

Emotional awareness – emotions carry important information

Aware: Emotions can be elusive
Warm up: *What are your most powerful feelings?*
Main question: *How do you notice and process emotional information?*

Engaged: Notice emotions as notifications
How do you prepare for conversations which may become emotional?
When is it productive to express emotions in the moment?

Empowered: Emotions include truth and direction
How do you sense and express emotions authentically?
How do you use emotional information in decision-making?

Note: Engaged and empowered level questions may be "homework" to process more deeply between coaching sessions.

How are you?

This common communication carries a heavy load and when not given due attention may cause more harm than good. Answers from fine to horrible may be elicited, and the inquiring person may not be prepared to respond meaningfully.

How are you? When this question is genuinely answered, it is a glimpse at the respondent's sense of well-being at that point in time. To answer, they likely think about notable things that happened during the day, whether their needs were met, interactions in which they were appreciated, respected, or successful, or opportunities to do their favorite things or see their favorite people. Well-being is fluid and dynamic. The variety of positive and possibly challenging experiences and thoughts occurring throughout each hour, day, week, or month impacts one's sense of well-being. The intensity of the experience and associated feelings impact the duration of the affect. Ask clients about their well-being at the start of a session to support their well-being and provide you with quality information on their state of mind for the work which will occur in the session.

Measure and monitor well-being

Overall well-being is an interaction between perceptions of and within different factors; safety, comfort, and success are key aspects of well-being. Figure 1.1 provides a simple ten step ladder to use as a scale for monitoring well-being. When well-being becomes diminished, awareness is the first step to restoring it. When well-being is strong, engagement safeguards it. Discussions which will add value to this include exploring what it means to be happy and healthy, describing factors which are important, unimportant, and even those that are unexplored.

Well-being factors

Coaching conversations about well-being and sense of self examine preferences and how they inform and impact the safety, comfort, or success aspects of well-being, or how preferences contribute to our overall sense of well-being. With your client, explore which specific areas are relevant to them, as an individual. Are they aware of and managing their preferences regarding safety? Are their stories about seeking comfort? Or perhaps their focus is on success, and they would benefit from discussions exploring their preferences related to accomplishment.

This is a perspective akin to Maslow's needs viewed using a lens of implicit development focused on perceptions. In our model, preferences interact as perceptual filters and develop to meet needs. Loosely speaking, we are concerned with safety and comfort to describe some of what Maslow categorized as basic and psychological needs; when considered the goal, once these are met, motivation decreases significantly. We are also focused on purpose and accomplishment, which are more closely related to Maslow's cognitive need which focuses on the need to understand the world; this area of need, even when met, is thought to increase motivation. As a side note, Perception Coaching® is not particularly concerned with the hierarchical aspect of Maslow's model.

Well-being refers to the dynamic states of mind, body, and being which influence feelings, what we do and think, as well as how we interact with the world. Starting with individual preferences we explore comfort and satisfaction with life, analogous to the basic and psychological needs in Maslow's hierarchy. Though safety, comfort, and accomplishment may be perceived to be linearly related, with safety being a basic need and accomplishment having a more abstract benefit, people can strive for safety when they have comfort or strive for accomplishment while risking safety. Individuals sharing an environment and experiencing similar situations likely perceive their own state of well-being differently as it depends on how their preferences regarding safety, comfort, and accomplishment influence their interpretation.

> Note: Physiological differences may result in one person being a little cold and another being a little warm in the same room. Also, one may prefer to be cold if being warm is the alternative, and vice-versa.
>   Many preferences may be informed by or stem from physiological differences; identifying the root cause of preference is not the goal of coaching. Coaches view preferences pragmatically and consider the implications of preferences with an eye to the future.

Safety and risk are instinctually considered with the goal of avoiding both physical and mental threats; this is an evolutionary default. Safety concerns are not the same as they were for our ancestors; survival was often threatened and physical safety was the primary goal. Now, material goods and finances are of great importance to many, and the desire to keep them safe extends our perceived need for safety beyond the self. People think about safety in many ways; there is physical safety, emotional safety, psychological safety, financial safety, safety of property, safety from threats, and numerous others. If something is valued, it is likely perceived to be at risk. Personal preferences are key to recognizing where safety is a factor in tensions, decisions, and filtering perceptual information.

When safety is of concern, risks are evaluated. Depending on the type and level of threat, emotions can range from positive excitement to paralyzing fear. Whether risk is accepted, pursued, or avoided is a context-dependent preference. Risk may be courageously or dumbly accepted, bravely or dangerously pursued, and risk avoidance may be wise or cowardly. When safety choices are judged in this manner, self-perception is similarly influenced.

Risk may be viewed as the other side of the safety coin. The goal of safety is to avoid loss and the goal of risk-taking is to gain rewards. Physical, financial, material, and psychological risks occur daily, in varying amounts. Some things of value may be worth the risk to attain or possibly maintain. Self-sabotage is generally an implicit risk assessment and reaction to threat. When behaviors considered to be self-sabotaging appear, discuss threats to well-being associated with the de-railed action or thinking to make them explicit and understood. Referral to a licensed professional is recommended if the threat or self-sabotaging behavior goes beyond the scope of coaching.

Unique personalities and experiences influence which traits, characteristics, and behaviors are perceived as safe. When traits, characteristics, and behaviors appear to keep us safe, they become preferred through a process of reinforcement. *Birds of a feather flock together* relates to the belief that if we look or behave similarly, we understand others in the group; the hypothesized understanding increases a sense of safety.

A welcoming community works for the greater good. Saying "hi" to a stranger you pass on the street is risky. These two perspectives are navigated by preferences. The possible rewards to greeting others may include the personal satisfaction of putting something positive out in the world, a returned greeting, or feeling a sense of connection or community. Risks are also numerous; you may be ignored, get a negative rebuttal, or even feel threatened by the stranger. Exploring multiple interpretations adds valuable insight. These perspectives shed some light on how two individuals may come to have wildly different perceptions when it comes to smiling at strangers. Neither is more valid than the other; they reflect perceptual impact.

Coaching practices

Social safety

The following question types are especially appropriate when client goals relate to prospecting, networking, empathy, and specific interpersonal skills.
Under what circumstances are you willing to say hi to a stranger?
*When would you **not** say hi to a stranger?*
Replace "say hi" with "give money" or "offer help" to explore client preferences for safety, risk, and prosocial behaviors with regards to places, people, and interactions.
Deeper analysis: *What potential biases do you perceive?*
Client conversations should include a variety of question topics to better explore and understand their preferences and concerns, and guide future conversations.

Comfort includes an absence of pain, stress, and tensions. Comfort is at risk if even the threat of discomfort is present. When comfort needs are met, it may include the presence of an ideal temperature, preferred food and drink, or enjoyable aesthetics or activities. Attention to comfort is the hallmark of a good host. They will notice if someone is chilly or too warm, needs a beverage, or seems ill at ease. Hosts often ask their guests "are you comfortable?" because comfort is memorable and tied to the experience. If someone's preferences for comfort are unmet, discomfort will be associated with the event, potentially causing future avoidance of the experience or host.

Like safety preference defaults, preferences related to comfort vary greatly by individual, and decisions naturally default to the alternative which is most comfortable. Emotional notifications also occur when comfort is the goal.

A person that is most comfortable with friends may feel uneasy or even resentful when a new person joins their group. A warm regard for others may be felt when one is seated in a favorite chair by their host and welcomed with smiles from other guests; in this moment they notice that they are very comfortable. When efforts to create physical and mental comfort cause discomfort, the objective becomes the focus. If a friend is giving you a ride and the car is too warm, multiple preferences impact responses. You may be direct: *Can I turn down the temperature?* Or casually mention, *It is warm in here.* Alternatively, one may feel grateful for the ride and that seems more important than the physical discomfort. Preferences for safety and comfort, including personal connections, also influence the manner of responding to emotional information; stronger preferences will elicit stronger emotions.

Preferences are important to explore; one aspect is how the client's preferences influence their efforts and goals. Comfort means we are in a state in which preferred needs are met. However, comfort is a limiting goal. Those who wish to reach stretch goals, increase their capacity, innovate, or be more authentically true to themselves analyze their preferences around comfort and benefit when they intentionally shift to accept some discomfort in their efforts to succeed.

Coaching practices

Efforts and goals

The conversation prompts below support critical analysis of the effort required to pursue a goal, potentially bolstering commitment to said goal. *What preferences related to safety and comfort do you set aside while taking productive risks?*
What goal do you have that is worth the discomfort of its pursuit?

Purpose and hope are keys to flourishing. Safety avoids loss, comfort includes preferences. To pursue purpose, productive risks are taken, and effort often leads to discomfort. That is not to say the well-being factors of purpose, comfort, and safety are mutually exclusive; these ideas exist with ambiguity which, when navigated, allow one to develop and change.

Well-being may be expressed in terms of need: I need something, I need more, or I need something different. For some safety is sufficient to create a sense of well-being and for others well-being may require success for the greater good, closely related to Maslow's higher needs of self-actualization and transcendence. Tensions among needs require objective consideration; emotional tensions arise when one strives for both comfort and accomplishment, simultaneously striving to mitigate threats while undertaking an endeavor which introduces risk. Coaches work with clients to establish coaching goals around meaningful areas of their lives; purpose creates resilience in the face of risks and becomes the focus of discussions, engagement, and purposeful work.

Success related to well-being is perceived differently by individuals; often success is achieved by obtaining safety and comfort. In performance coaching, purpose aligns with Maslow's version of the elusive self-actualization. Success as a reflection of well-being includes feeling valued and respected, learning and developing, and belonging to something greater than oneself. Clients come to coaching to find support to meet a specific goal or because they sense a need they cannot meet or perhaps even identify. Exploring clients' perspectives related to success is essential to coach–client relationships.

Bias box

Needs and risk

Coaching which supports focus on purpose leads to flourishing more effectively than responding to emotionally charged needs.

Well-being preferences are implicitly developed and guide thinking, relating, and ways of doing. When out in the world with others or alone reflecting on the day, emotions function as an alert system for the state of well-being. Emotions bring attention to information that is relevant to our preferences, especially safety, comfort, and purpose which navigate needs and risk.

Safety: Attention to safety is the perceptual default; our senses are constantly scanning features of the environment to evaluate the possibilities of risk or threat. This evolutionary purpose ensures survival and meets needs at a basic level.

How do you feel when you sense risk? Preferences regarding safety guide attention and when safety is the primary goal, emotional responses are triggered when threats are detected. Sense of self is influenced by feelings related to safety.

Comfort: When comfort is the goal, one seeks a predictable environment where preferences are met; risk is not generally tolerated. It is evident that comfort is preferred when one immediately acts to change the situation when faced with discomfort.

A decision about going to a movie or watching a movie at home is informed by comfort. How might each place be comfortable? Is a little discomfort worth being among the first to see it?

Purpose: Pursuing purpose includes inherent risks, including the possibility of failure. Attention is drawn to goal-relevant features and information, even in the presence of risks to safety.

Do you have a goal you are willing to pursue despite possible risks? When one is willing to risk safety and comfort for a goal, it is a worthy purpose.

Explore your preferences in the area of needs. For each pair mark the strength of your preference between the two anchors; the center is neutral, indicating no preference.

Safety ---- 3 ---- 2 ---- 1 ---- 0 ---- 1 ---- 2 ---- 3 ---- **Comfort**
Safety ---- 3 ---- 2 ---- 1 ---- 0 ---- 1 ---- 2 ---- 3 ---- **Purpose**
Comfort ---- 3 ---- 2 ---- 1 ---- 0 ---- 1 ---- 2 ---- 3 ---- **Purpose**

Note the order and strength of your preferences.

Reflect and discuss

Consider the purpose, values, and benefits of the three areas of need:

1. Describe circumstance or environment for which attention should:

    •   remain the default of safety
    •   center on comfort
    •   be directed to find purpose or goal information.

2. Considering how each area of need functions, do you naturally follow the path toward safety, comfort, or purpose? Explain.
3. How does this preference set contribute to your coaching perspective?

Manage emotions: Decisions and tension

Because emotions are rooted in experience, preferences, and perceptions, individuals have varying emotional response styles for any given topic or event. There is likely an emotional response when one is offered an opportunity to skydive, especially if this extreme endeavor is not an everyday experience. It may elicit positive excitement: *Yes, please!* Alternatively, it may trigger a response of *No, never!* Both emotional responses stop cognitive processes. Strong emotional responses indicate strong preferences and pose an opportunity to widen perceptions and see more possibilities through examination. Alternatively, it may truly be a decision if a strong gut reaction doesn't preempt cognitive opportunity, becoming a decision where benefits and risks are actively weighed to make an informed choice.

Client One had been casually monitoring job openings and was randomly offered an opportunity to work in a competing firm. They came in for a decision session and described their choices like this: I can take the risky path which is going for the new job or the smart path which is staying where I am. My first *thought* was: It seems they already decided. My first *question* was: What is your immediate preference? Their response: "None, that is why I came to you." It seems they did not intend to start the discussion with bias. Bringing to light the value laden descriptors, *risky* and *smart*, supports suspending judgment, as well as more objective discussions and reflection. Though no emotional words were used, what needs and preferences may be sensed in the way they expressed the choices? What tensions might exist among their needs for safety, comfort, and accomplishment?

Emotions are a product of our experience, preferences, and perceptions and tend to simultaneously influence and reinforce those characteristics. Noticing and exploring emotions provides a unique opportunity to develop insights related to preferences and perceptions.

When addressing overall well-being, it is also important to understand strategies clients may use to manage their emotions. Some situations are charged with emotion, if too powerful, barriers develop. Strong negative emotions are red flags/notifications which require attention. Strong positive emotions also warrant attention. Expressing them inappropriately may be problematic, and they might be useful to understand related attitudes.

Coaching practices

Responding to strong emotions

Clients concerned with strong emotions likely process them in coaching. They may also benefit from strategies to defuse and process their feelings more immediately.

In the moment strategies require rehearsal. Clients will select one they are drawn to and imagine using it. Then when it is needed, they are more likely to be able to activate it.

Think about a time you could have used one of these strategies and practice it in your head.

In the moment

Count to 10 (diverts attention and emotion can begin to dissipate)
Step back (figuratively, and possibly physically)
Notice what happened right before the emotion:

- *What were you doing?*
- *Who was present?*
- *What were they doing?*

The *notice* strategy supports "becoming an onlooker" to focus on *identifying triggers, understanding* the emotion, *avoiding magnifying,* or *preparing* for emotions.

After the emotion

Acknowledge the emotion as a notification of something significant
    Recenter by viewing the emotional trigger from different perspectives
    Reframe the situation to

- *access grace*
- *lead with positive intent*
- *plan a difficult conversation.*

Once strong emotions dissipate somewhat, discuss the alerted or offended belief or preference to determine its relevance and validity.
    How is the trigger directly related and important to this situation?
    How does this belief still serve you?

Coaching practices

Improve self-concept – prioritize authenticity

Emotions can function as notifications that your self-concept or preferences have been dismissed or offended; explore them to support your authenticity.

Aware: Emotions are experienced and expressed in many ways
Warm up: *What are your most powerful feelings?*
Main question: *What range of emotions do you regularly experience?*

Engaged: Experience, recognize, and express emotions
What emotions do you share? Are there emotions you hide?
What can you learn from the emotions of others?
How does your emotional expression support your authentic self?

Empowered: Align your experienced and expressed emotions for authenticity
How does showing authentic emotion build trust?
In what ways will you nurture your authentic presence?

Note: Engaged and empowered level questions may be "homework" to process more deeply between coaching sessions.

Navigate life with others

5

Goal: Healthy interactions with others; psychological and emotional safety.

Efforts: Lead with positive intent, build trust, be authentic.

Exploring perceptions in the Watercolor Class vignette, we saw how Terry and Charlie advocated for safety and comfort by their focus when they entered the room. Upon entering the room, each ensured they had some level of safety based on their needs. The plan to meet there likely also increased their sense of safety.

Unlike this example of Terry and Charlie, people are not always aware of what they need to feel safe or comfortable, and they may also struggle with making decisions that help them get what they need. Even in the Watercolor Class example, there may have been tension.

Research has shown that people have a need to belong; it makes them feel safe. Tensions increase when needs or preferences are at odds with one another. For instance, if Charlie has an intention to greet everyone to feel a part of the larger community, this is interrupted when they notice Terry, with whom they want to visit. Charlie has competing preferences. They want to have a meaningful conversation with Terry; this takes time. Not connecting with the others in the room feels uncomfortable for Charlie, which grows if an opportunity is not found to complete that task in a timely manner. Additionally, if Charlie's passion for community also fuels the mission to greet every person, to make each one feel welcome, they may become frustrated or worried, causing them to be less attentive in the conversation with Terry. Now Charlie is failing in both intentions.

DOI: 10.4324/9781003332770-7

Sense of self is a deep topic of exploration; it becomes more complex as we, like Terry and Charlie, begin to interact and look for ways to meet our own needs and work to support others.

Coaching practices

Authenticity – emotional awareness and expression are aligned

Start with awareness. *When do you share your feelings with others?*

Aware: Feelings are notifications for yourself and others
Warm up: *What feelings are easiest to express to others?*
Main question: *What influences your ability to express feelings authentically?*

Engaged: Others sense authenticity when emotions are expressed
What emotions can you share to help others understand you better?
How will you navigate emotions to express them productively?

Empowered: Emotions motivate, inform, and build trust
How will emotions provide motivation for yourself or help others understand your purpose?
What emotions should you be sharing to inform others?
How will authentic emotional expression develop trust?

Note: Engaged and empowered level questions may be "homework" to process more deeply between coaching sessions.

Reflecting on one's experiences is enriched by perspective development which includes *considering alternative interpretations of* one's experiences, preferences, and attitudes. This process explores inward; to further develop perspective consider others' experiences, preferences, and attitudes as unique and valuable points of view, relative to and as well as your own. Social-emotional learning explores ways individual preferences impact people navigating life together and contributes insights to understand means to interact for the best results.

Sense of self in social situations

Understanding preferences and how they interact with needs provides a powerful start to developing well-being. Next level development includes actively learning while being who you are, doing what you can do, and advocating for what you value, in other words *living authentically*. This aspect of the elusive self-actualization is reliant on feeling a sense of psychological and emotional safety. Often perceived threats get in the way of authenticity. The cloud of doubt – *What will others think?* and more to the point *Will **being myself** hurt my reputation or potential?* – often causes individuals to have multiple personas for different situations. This variability limits one's ability to be authentic. Simultaneously, though perhaps a contradiction, safety and comfort are maintained by flexible responses because expectations vary by environment and are best met with different response patterns.

Advocate for well-being

Injuries are important to understand and prevent. Though physical injuries can be obvious and traumatic, they are not the only type of threat to well-being. The subtlety of emotional and psychological safety in work and social environments has a great impact on well-being. Understanding needs and advocating for them so that everyone can bring their authentic self is the most powerful strategy set we have for improving well-being for individuals and organizations.

Life is fine

From work to volunteering and dining with friends, one likely responds to *how was your day?* in many ways.

If your day started with an empty coffee container, you couldn't find your wallet, and the bus didn't stop when you signaled it, you may be a little flustered and a simple, "How is your day going?" will likely elicit different responses relevant to the situation.

At work you may say *fine* and not share freely if you are up for promotion and feel the details may jeopardize your chances, or you may share details to express why you are distracted.

If you volunteer at a homeless shelter, you may say *fine* because you do not want to sound like a complainer, or you may share your relative discomfort with newfound perspective.

If you are dining with friends, you may say *fine*, or you might authentically share your morning experience, worry about the promotion, and the new perspective you found.

Fine is a safe response to common inquiries like *How was your day?* Safety over authenticity limits potential for connecting with others.

Safety as a priority may be intentional in a culture which is competitive, predatory, or combative; or it may be unintentional, done automatically without awareness because it is comfortable and *works for you.*

Experiencing psychological and emotional safety is like being with best friends; one has the ability to behave authentically without fear of loss of reputation, credibility, position, or potential opportunities. Additionally, when safety is expected, one feels included and able to take risks to challenge the status quo, learn from mistakes, and share feelings. Fear of loss and willingness to take risks capture two ends of the safety continuum. Like many dichotomies, there are likely seasons in which rules of thumb suggest one moves from one extreme to the other, over time.

An early career retirement fund is often invested in higher risk funds which are likely to have a higher return, with the mindset that losses can be regained over time. Closer to retirement, investments are more often in low-risk areas, creating small gains, so as not to jeopardize goals. In the retirement scenario, it is recommended that investments move on the continuum from high risk to low risk, over time. This is statistically sound, but individuals have preferences which influence how comfortable they are with risk and saving. Some individuals are risk avoidant and prefer low risk with low return for the safety of their savings from day one. Others may embrace risk and continue higher risk investments right up to retirement. In their lottery study Sokolowska et al. (2021) discovered when given nine opportunities 25% of respondents selected zero to two risky choices, preferring risk avoidance, and 27% selected seven to nine risky choices, this latter group being categorized as risk prone. The remaining participants could not be easily categorized, though likely fall into middle ground, perhaps mediating risk. Similarly, individual differences exist regarding social safety.

The wonderful thing about statistics and any rule of thumb is that they suggest an informed starting point for finding ways to meet the needs of individuals. Individual differences like those observed in talent and risk tolerance research enrich the world, make things interesting, and confound a rule of thumb, preventing generalized strategies from effectively meeting the needs of all individuals.

Bias box

Individual differences

Understand preferences to facilitate shifting perceptions and reducing biases and develop sense of self and sense of others.

People have limited ability to sense other perspectives, even when they find alternative points of view to be interesting, powerful, and helpful to fulfill diverse individual and societal needs. Recognizing preferences as opinions has the power to break down barriers. Explore the operationalization of preferences toward bias and perspective.

Preference: One's normal approach or often selected means of proceeding. Evaluation is related to self; this is my best way to address the need. Preferences are developed when related choices contribute to the holder's purpose. Approaches are neutral and may be used productively or they may create challenges or barriers.

Talents are an example of preferred ways of doing, thinking, or relating. Others' talents and related preferences are valid and valuable, appreciating this is an essential aspect of safeguarding and promoting authenticity.

Bias: One is confident their preference is the best approach or most effective or useful way of doing; their preferred approach is beneficial for nearly every situation and other ideas are wrong and other approaches are deficient. The strength of the related preferences causes these opinions to become barriers to alternatives.

Unexamined preferences and ideas are more likely to be operationalized as biases. When preferences act as a protective barrier, they become biases which support choices and actions deemed safe or predictable.

Perspective: One recognizes that their preference is one approach of many possible approaches. Judgment or evaluation of other approaches is suspended, and when appropriate is related to the specific person and context of the situation.

With perspective, preferences act as a starting point from which to see more or other approaches. This provides a means to find common ground, understand differences, and bridge gaps in understanding; then those with complementary approaches can appreciate each other and navigate challenges.

Self-assess

Think about which understanding benefits your intentions to impact perceptions. For each pair mark the strength of your preference between the two anchors; the center is neutral, indicating no preference.

Preference ---- 3 ---- 2 ---- 1 ---- 0 ---- 1 ---- 2 ---- 3 ---- **Bias**
Preference ---- 3 ---- 2 ---- 1 ---- 0 ---- 1 ---- 2 ---- 3 ---- **Perspective**
Perspective ---- 3 ---- 2 ---- 1 ---- 0 ---- 1 ---- 2 ---- 3 ---- **Bias**

Note the order and strength of your preferences.

Reflect and discuss

Consider the purpose, values, and benefits of the three approaches to thinking about lived opinions.

1. Describe when exploring each is most beneficial:

   - Preference
   - Bias
   - Perspective

2. Both bias and perspective are rooted in preferences.

   a. How is choice related to preferences?
   b. How is choice relevant when discussing naturally or implicitly developed talents?

3. Do you see other factors that you could add to this bias box?
4. How does this content contribute to your coaching perspective?

Prosocial motivation

There is a benefit to helping others which is greater than the help provided. Prosocial behaviors include decisions and actions that benefit others, including ensuring psychological-emotional safety and comfort. Perception Coaching® has roots in positive psychology and encourages improved well-being through the good put into the world by prosocial behaviors.

It is important to note, individuals do things that benefit others for a variety of reasons. Serving the needs of others makes people feel good, while for some, helping others may be a by-product of helping themselves; these motives are both seen as egoism. Perhaps one is acting solely to benefit someone, or a group; these may be seen as altruism and collectivism, respectively. Finally, one may be motivated to help others by a greater mission or principle. The reasons and theories are as diverse as the acts, more likely as diverse as the actors.

Because motivation may be clouded by the motivational theories and individual differences, Batson (2022) suggests using a Galilean approach, appreciating the strengths and weaknesses of the motives so that one may focus on bringing prosocial behaviors forward. Regardless of motivation, or maybe in support of diverse motivations, implementing prosocial behaviors has the potential to improve individual well-being, as well as interpersonal relationships. Awareness of how others are perceived is an area of great opportunity in efforts to increase prosocial approaches.

Perceiving others

Immediate perceptions of others are made without our awareness and have implications for if and how we interact with individuals both unknown and known to us. When someone is making wild gestures, they may be perceived as dramatic. The first impression gathered by someone with an intolerance for emotional drama would likely be different than that of someone driving an emergency vehicle.

How do spontaneous perceptions change or update? Olcaysoy Okten et al. (2019) studied first impressions through the lens of trait and evaluative inferences. Attention is drawn to wild gesturing which elicits spontaneous perceptual inferences. The study gave particular attention to impressions using a short description and how first impression perceptions change with more information, for example wild gesturing may be used to get the attention of the driver in an emergency vehicle. The initial bystander inference may have been about the drama; how might an explanatory contingency alter the meaning of their perception? In their study, Olcaysoy Okten et al. provided a stem behavior to all participants and half received, after a delay, a contingency with potential to transform the gist of the stem. Both trait and evaluative inferences were spontaneously drawn by participants; the contingency information tended to influence implicit evaluative inferences though not implicit trait inferences.

Further study uncovered that though the initial trait inference did not update, a separate trait inference was created based on the stem and contingency. In their discussion, authors differentiated their study of spontaneous perceptions from those of intentional perceptions which lead to stereotypes, though similar patterns may exist. The robustness of trait inferences may be explained by the attention and processing required to change this type of inference. The robustness of initial implicit inferences lends a sense of immediacy for implementing strategies which support positive perceptual shifts, especially when related to people.

Coaching practices

Seeing others – expand perceptual filters to reduce assumptions

Start with awareness. *What traits or characteristics do you look for in others?*

Aware: Similarities help us understand the world simplistically
Warm up: *What can someone's appearance tell you?*
Main questions: *What information is important when you meet someone? How have first impressions influenced relation building? What traits or characteristics do you look for in others?*

Are there people you have met that you have avoided because of first impressions? What qualities or "red flags" do you tend to avoid?

Engaged: First impressions are powerful and limited; replace judgment with curiosity
What is important to and for you? What do you want people to know about you?
What questions might you ask someone you first meet to see them more authentically?

Empowered: Recognize the complexity of the human condition and avoid judgment
How does living with ambiguity support suspending judgment?
What overt attention or action helps to navigate first impressions and appreciate the complexity of others?

Note: Engaged and empowered level questions may be "homework" to process more deeply between coaching sessions.

Strategies to suspend judgment use intentional means to update spontaneous evaluative inferences regarding individuals; this is a powerful first step to mediate first impressions and improve interpersonal skills and relationships.

Suspending judgment addresses the goal of safety, including awareness to lead with positive intent and support mutual high regard. Because individuals have varying needs, start with questions rather than assumptions. No matter how statistically robust your assertion may be, when others respond to you their expression of their perspective engages them and you more powerfully. For emotional and psychological safety consider the limitations of rules of thumb and first impressions, and instead start developing deep trust so that authenticity, learning, and advocacy thrive, as a prosocial approach.

Lead with positive intent

Navigating is how one chooses to respond to circumstances. This does not happen in isolation; one must somehow arrive at that moment, and plan to continue after that moment. Our next strategy is especially relevant in that it is used *in the moment* to connect with others to begin relieving tension. When implemented as a way of doing, leading with positive intent contributes to strong relationships that can withstand future tensions and conflict and is a way of doing that is essential to coaching as well as relationships. It requires putting one's interests and concerns aside when addressing others; this is not a natural stance for most people.

Innate preferences influence socialization. One's own interests and motives are naturally at work when interacting with others. This poses something of a tension when paired with the ideas that people have autonomy and are valued and appreciated for who they are. To lead with positive intent requires awareness of one's own perspectives and needs because they must often be set aside to avoid manipulation and using others as a means to an end. It is an approach which exemplifies *no strings attached.*

In roles of parent, guardian, caregiver, educator, or social support, treating those you serve as autonomous individuals can be difficult. The purpose of these roles naturally leads one to directing, correcting, and reinforcing the behaviors of an otherwise autonomous individual. Often, the support given in these roles is done from the perspective of the relationship or organization, moving the individual effectively within or through a system. When rationales given for the task are *because I'm the mom* or *you need this to get to the next thing,* the individual's needs are likely not front of mind nor treated as relevant. To lead with positive intent, shift to the perspective of the person with whom you are working and consider how the work directly benefits them. The efforts may be similar, but interactions will increasingly shift to positive intent as focus remains on the needs of the person receiving support. The rationales become *because this provides you valuable experience, how would you like to do it? Or this is the usual next step people take to meet the objective you set for yourself, unless you see another way?* This shift increases relevance for the individual, trust that someone values their efforts, and awareness that the process or system will be of benefit to the individual.

Coaching practices

Giving as positive intent

Aware: The benefits of giving
Warm up: *Why do you give gifts?*
Main question: *What are the benefits of giving?*

Engaged: Understand intentions and benefits
When giving gifts, what is your hope?
What is the purpose of giving cash?

Empowered: Shift intention from perspective of self to that of another
How does the gift benefit the receiver?
How do you ensure the gift you give is wanted?

Note: Engaged and empowered level questions may be "homework" to process in context or more deeply between sessions.

Build trust and relieve tensions

In social and work situations, tensions often arise from unspoken expectations. People expect a lot from each other, much of which seems unnecessary to explain. Clarifying even "obvious" expectations is beneficial because, as we explored, individuals have very different ideas of what they need and can provide; expectations have similarly variable interpretations.

I need to feel respected. I want respect. Everyone deserves respect. Each statement expresses different expectations relating to respect, with little clarity on how respect is defined or shown. Appreciating different perspectives leads to authentic conversations and questions to better understand expectations, intentions, and each other, which naturally builds trust.

In teams this is especially important and ideally occurs in formalized norm setting discussions when the team is formed. In his 1965 literature review, Tuckman discusses stage 1 testing and dependence, stage 2 intragroup conflict, stage 3 group cohesion, and stage 4 functional goal relatedness. Though the previous are more descriptive, you likely are familiar with the more memorable stages of form, storm, norm, and perform. This stage model functions as our reference point for social interactions more generally.

New social interactions are often optimistic and involve observations which help those involved sense how they may engage; these feelings and behaviors also occur when groups or teams form. There may even be a sense of leadership bestowed on the individual who initiated the interaction or gathering. With familiarity, tensions may develop and individuals may push boundaries and storming occurs. If the tensions are addressed, differences are resolved and better understanding and trust develop; the norming phase is reached. Much like self-actualization, the final stage of performing is accomplished with effort. All involved are engaged in social interactions, individual differences are appreciated as sources of perspective and strength, and trust is expected and given to all.

The stage-based approach is useful as a model for building trust. One may anticipate the "honeymoon period" which accompanies forming new connections; the future is imagined based on the small sample of (hopefully) authentic behaviors. As relationships develop one begins to perceive preferences, especially as opportunities arise for different authentic behaviors to occur; this is the point when the unexpected may be experienced. Tension is created to protect safety or comfort and trust suddenly seems to drop; it is beneficial to reflect to determine if an incorrect assumption is undermining trust.

Discussions around preferences improve trust, because sharing beliefs, talents, values, and other preferences reduce the unknowns which create assumptions. When this is done proactively, norms develop more quickly and trust is supported. The speed of trust is also a preference. Some individuals trust immediately, for others trustworthiness is earned. In any team or relationship, if unexplored the variability of this may impact the social experience.

Appreciating others and safeguarding their sense of self contributes to an environment where authenticity flourishes. For those who don't naturally do it, navigating differences feels awkward, requiring one to shift from understanding others using automatic, implicit assumptions to interactively working with others to understand them. Storming as a phase in social group development is borne out of individuals seeking to be recognized, to be understood, and to contribute. When this happens, everyone can perform by interacting authentically.

Coaching practices

Create an atmosphere for authenticity

Recognize attributes of climate and culture which support your preferences and authenticity, as well as those of others.
When are you happiest?

- *What are you doing?*
- *Who is there?*

What are your preferences when it comes to socializing?

- *Group events?*
- *One-to-one interactions?*

To what environments are you drawn?
What factors support authentic behaviors?
How does situational awareness support authenticity?
How do expectations limit authentic behaviors?
When preferences are diverse, discuss and set norms that appreciate differences so people can coexist and be valued authentically.

Reflect and discuss

Well-being is essential for individuals and communities.

1. How might you broach an aspect of this subject with someone who is struggling to find fulfillment?

2. Would you start every client with a session exploring well-being? Why *and* why not?
3. Refer to Appendix Table A.1; select a client profile.

    a. What questions might you pose regarding psychological and emotional safety?
    b. What indicates an opportunity to explore relationships?

Navigate work with others

Working in teams or other group arrangements adds factors which, when compared to individual considerations, can increase perspective, support, and engagement. Work groups also may threaten safety and comfort. Work environments can feel predictable because often purpose and expectations are clearer than social situations. Simultaneously, work provides parameters and situations which may feel restrictive, making one feel stuck in unsafe or uncomfortable relationships.

Collaborative relationships and teams

Collaboration is a means to improve both working conditions and results. Complementary partners are those who have the same purpose and different approaches, talents, and perspectives, whereas similar partners have alignment with some or all factors. Both complementary partners and those with similarities can work in harmony, valuing mutual support and progress. However, in an environment in which participants do not feel valued, collaboration can cause tension, distrust, and undermine productivity.

Authentic discussions around individual talents and needs followed by norm setting improves outcomes in collaborative spaces. Team development phases are useful to understanding collaborative relationships. New teams who take time to establish norms move more quickly to become high performing. Whenever a team gains or loses a member, reset the foundations as a new team to bring the new member up to speed or close the gap left by a departing member.

Norms and culture

The things for which a group is known describe the group's culture. Collaborative norm setting is useful to establish behavioral expectations and set the tone for meetings and general interactions.

New teams benefit from norm setting; in the forming phase teams are "artificially aligned" as individuals observe and acquiesce, as they determine their place on the team. Thoughtful and intentional norm setting done early helps the group meet the safety and comfort needs of all members before individual preferences can be inadvertently offended. Norms also clarify and support behaviors which contribute to the purpose of the group.

That team has a system for hearing everyone's voices. This is a norm, and it likely demonstrates that the team agrees valuing all members ideas is important.

Roles and responsibilities

Roles provide a system for creating clear, manageable expectations. Collaborative partners and teams often distribute responsibilities to reduce redundancy and allow individuals to do what they do best. Someone who sees the big picture may lead, another who includes others may facilitate, another who always takes notes may edit them to be useful to the team, yet another may be a time-minder, while the whole team keeps the focus topic front and center.

Team responsibilities and duties consider individual, team, and role-specific tasks. When responsibilities are integrated in this manner, time and resources are more effectively allocated to support team efforts. When team responsibilities have poor to no alignment with individual members' duties, one or the other is likely neglected. Teams which function to support members' efforts by eliminating unnecessary duplication, sharing expertise and strategies, and providing complementary partners become high performers.

Performance

High performing teams are exceptionally engaged and appear to have fluid roles, collaborate to focus efforts, and ensure interactions support the psychological safety of all members. Performance is enhanced by dynamically leveraging both individual and team talents. Team talents are derived from synergistic talent elements – specific members' talents combining to create a whole greater than the sum of the parts. The apparently fluid roles are the result of effective communication in an atmosphere of mutual appreciation, understanding, and trust.

Coaching practices

Interpersonal skills – working with similarities and differences

Start with awareness. *Are you drawn to similarities or differences?*

Aware: Both similarities and differences exist among all individuals
Warm up: *Think of a close friend, how are they similar to you? How are they different?*
Main question: *What helps you understand ways in which you are similar to and different from others?*

Engaged: Seek to understand and appreciate others
What do you appreciate about individual differences?
How does understanding similarities support collaboration?

Empowered: Awareness of relevant approaches and values
How do relevant similarities and differences interact in your team?
What similarities or differences are less relevant and may distract the team?
What processes support individuals to authentically contribute to the team?

Note: Engaged and empowered level questions may be "homework" to process more deeply between coaching sessions.

Leading an organization

Direct and delegate

Leadership takes many forms, all of which benefit from clarity of purpose paired with understanding staff; aligning purpose and staff preferences is a path to success for the leader and their team. Managers may lead teams generally through directing staff based on individual and team roles and responsibilities. Executives likely lead managers and directors by delegating duties based on clear goals for their departments or in their areas of expertise.

Vision and expectations

Imagining and planning for an *ideal goal state* for a team or organization requires both vision and a clear understanding of what is possible. Clear expectations create a path forward as the ideal future is pursued. To effectively lead, clear communication of the vision supports follower engagement.

Delegating is a means to develop or elevate a direct report which is especially effective when they are inspired by the vision; a clear goal is provided and the means to complete it are up to the delegate. This means of assigning work or tasks requires leaders to understand and appreciate direct reports' preferences for engagement and facing challenges as it creates an opportunity for staff members to take on more responsibility, use their talents, and experience more autonomy in their roles.

Strategy and plans

The ability to orchestrate a strategy and plan for a team or organization requires expertise in current systems and processes as well as problem solving. Strategic leaders sense patterns and work to create or improve systems to be more effective and efficient. Leading and managing others in this area includes directing when the path or process is established and staff are, or can be, trained to complete the task as directed.

Directing is especially beneficial when a leader recognizes staff preferences related to implementing the process. Purposeful selection of a team or individual staff member ensures engagement and achievement. The limitations to the staff's autonomy when they are directed are notable because the process is often well-defined. However, should issues arise, aligned talents safeguard productivity.

Feedback and support

Both directing and delegating must include clear expectations to make effective feedback possible. Whether expectations are met, unmet, or partially met, providing feedback improves performance.

Interacting with others effectively increases well-being and meets needs. Immediate feedback informed by performance and expectations is especially beneficial for staff. If giving effective feedback is difficult, expectations should be revisited to determine if progress or success in meeting expectations can be made explicit. What does acceptable performance look like? What might indicate unacceptable performance? The nature of the task may indicate a scale related to acceptable performance which may also include exemplary performance.

A successful leader creates ways to support staff challenged to meet high expectations for performance. Support for well-being and performance comes in many forms and should align with the challenges staff members face. Support may include training for knowledge and procedural gaps, teaching, if decision or reasoning skills need to be developed, and coaching to address development of individual or team talents or preferences.

Coaching practice

Leadership – navigating purpose with others' well-being in mind

Aware: Tensions and stress
Warm up: *What causes you stress as a leader?*
Main question: *How do you see the needs of your followers?*

Engaged: Decision-making includes others
How do you make decisions?
What stages of decision-making benefit from diverse perspectives?
In what ways do your followers influence your decisions?

Empowered: Clear communication meets everyone's needs
How do you provide the right information to your followers?
What communication systems are in place between you and your team?
How do you ensure access and transparency for effective leadership?

Note: Engaged and empowered level questions may be "homework" to process more deeply between coaching sessions.

Bias box

Leadership focus

Effectively directing and delegating followers is the most powerful skill-set a leader delivers.

Leadership can be formal or informal, role related, and the result of an individual's presence. Regardless of its origin, to be effective, the leader likely has talents or preferences which include vision, strategy, or influencing others.

Vision and expectations: Imagining a future for a group or organizations requires forward thinking directed at purpose and mission. Unthought of potential and unique solutions bolster this and lend specifics which create expectations for that future.

Visions can be the result of seeking to meet unmet needs or making a good organization great. One may think: *What would it look like if our products were accessible to all?*

Strategy and plans: Understanding all of the "moving parts" in an organization requires expert knowledge of systems and how they interact.

The leader who prefers this focus is a problem solver and imagines how changes may affect staff in diverse roles to improve implementation.

Strategies likely change current practices. *What processes need to be created or put into place to fulfill our vision? How will these affect stakeholders?*

Direct and delegate: Influence is the key word in this leadership area, which focuses on implementation. The leader especially adept at finding the right people for the role or task to be done is successful; when direct reports are working in preferred ways, they are engaged and appreciate the leadership which supports them. When a leader directs others, staff follow their instructions to complete the work. Delegation results in staff taking responsibility to determine the best path and complete the work.

Influencing implementation ideally aligns preferences and competencies of followers. Leaders who direct and delegate know the members of their team, their talents, and their needs. *Who can navigate stakeholder needs to find the best solution? Who is the best person to implement this process?*

Self-assess

Which aspect of leadership is easiest for you to consider? For each pair mark the strength of your preference between the two anchors; the center is neutral, indicating no preference.

Vision ---- 3 ---- 2 ---- 1 ---- 0 ---- 1 ---- 2 ---- 3 ---- Strategy
Vision ---- 3 ---- 2 ---- 1 ---- 0 ---- 1 ---- 2 ---- 3 ---- Influence
Influence ---- 3 ---- 2 ---- 1 ---- 0 ---- 1 ---- 2 ---- 3 ---- Strategy

Note the order and strength of your preferences.

Reflect and discuss

Consider the purpose, values, and benefits of the three areas:

1. Describe the circumstances when supporting well-being improves:

    *   engaging others to understand vision and expectations
    *   others' access to a leader's strategy and plans
    *   effectively influencing and supporting direct reports.

2. The potential impact of leadership is great. How do you support leadership through the steps, from seeing a potential future to engaging and supporting the organization through implementation?
3. How does this contribute to your coaching perspective?

Performance coaching

PART
3

DOI: 10.4324/9781003332770-8

Productivity and cognitive-behavioral development

The first section of Part 3 focuses on successfully understanding the world to discover possibilities for effectively applying talents to learning and other applications in the context of productivity. Discussion explores understanding skills and motivation as essential factors of productivity which can be understood with authentic curiosity, then effectively developed.

Cognitive-behavioral development acknowledges that when talents and preferences show up, they can contribute to and inhibit progress. Development includes clarifying task expectations, both behavioral and cognitive, and focusing on the right talents and skills to successfully plan and perform productively. Coaches support clients' alignment of talents and preferences with the cognitive and behavioral expectations related to goal tasks or roles.

Innovation and opportunity-hypotheses development

The roles of ideation, experimentation, and expertise in innovation and success are discussed in these chapters. Growth is enhanced by focus on a hope for the future, sometimes perceived as a barrier or challenge to overcome.

Opportunity-hypotheses development supports clients' curiosity and creativity as means to see opportunities and address especially stubborn goals. Generating hypotheses and *what if* questions integrate creative ideas and clients' experiences. These are used to predict potential actions and outcomes as an exercise or planning tool.

As you explore Part 3, keep your coach perspective in mind; recognize both the potential and limitations of the topic areas outlined. The areas are comprehensive for Perception Coaching®, while leaving space for connections and other goals. Consider areas you prefer, in which you have or desire to develop expertise; perhaps there is a goal topic which does not seem to be addressed. These may indicate a niche area for you as a coach. Make the content your own by continuing to add these and your own relevant questions and strategies to your toolbox.

Productivity and cognitive-behavioral development

6

Goal: Make progress, perform, get things done.

Efforts: Cognitive-behavioral development; activate relevant preferences and develop strategies and expertise to succeed.

Cognitive and behavioral development focuses on efficiency and effectiveness related to how to think, relate, and do.

I just need to make progress!

Sometimes a client has what appears to be a very clear goal, such as the client who started their first coaching session with: *I am a doctoral student and have been for a few years. I work full time and have a family and really want to find a way to make progress on my dissertation.* There is a lot of information in two short, clear sentences. **Tell me more** is a great prompt to determine if the client has tried strategies, wants to address specific needs, or knows how they want coaching to support their efforts.

Some clients need their coach to begin to help them filter their experiences or goal. When a client has a full schedule, there are many approaches available. Productivity requires time and effort. Exploring each of these with the client may be beneficial. Time preferences are influenced by expectations for timeline, urgency, and ultimately one's sense of autonomy. Is there flexibility to find the best or most appropriate time for the task? Autonomy regarding effort and how the task is completed also contributes to productivity. Is there choice regarding how the task is done, so that one may engage their preferences in the effort?

DOI: 10.4324/9781003332770-9

Coaching practices

Productivity check list

Aware: The task is clear
What are the expectations related to this task?
Do you have the skills and resources to complete the task?

Engaged: Talents and efforts contribute to success
How is your effort toward this goal meaningful?
Which preferences are met as you work to accomplish the task?

Empowered: Autonomy regarding decision-making and progress
What happens when a barrier or challenge appears?
What is the scope of the work; what are the next steps?

Set and clarify missions or goals

Identifying the purpose and details of long-term missions, short-term goals, and other projects takes valuable time, yet when included in goal planning this analysis increases focus and efficiency. A goal with sufficient complexity or barriers warrants clarification; strategically defining purpose as the first step in planning is a time investment which pays off by making needs, priorities, and resources clear before investing effort.

Coaching practices

Organize goals and tasks

Start with awareness. *How do you determine the tasks you do daily?*

Aware: Daily life is busy; balance small and large expectations.
Warm up: *What is on your list of things to do?*
Main question: *How do you find time to accomplish expectations?*

Engaged: Organize your to do list.
What items are routine tasks?
What type of scheduling or checklist helps with these tasks?
Which things on your list are important projects?
What subgoals contribute to each project?

Empowered: Explicit planning prevents immediacy from displacing intention.
What type of habit or ritual contributes to efficient routine tasks?
Which important projects are your priority? Why?

Needs and opportunities

Decision-making is an essential productivity skill. How does one determine what should be done, and where effort should be directed? There are many ways to select tasks; bring the following perspectives to coaching conversations to support clients' efforts to select with intention.

Individuals who first accomplish tasks that appear to be easiest or most straightforward may come to coaching because they feel like they are always busy and not making progress. *Ready, fire, aim* is a metaphor for productivity in which "taking action" appears to be the goal. Action is truly only productive when it is intentionally aimed at worthwhile and meaningful goals; this sentiment shows a bias for goal-setting. Identifying preferences related to productivity is useful to align beliefs, talents, and attitudes, to reduce the energy, and focus the efforts required to accomplish progress.

Mark Twain has suggested strategies for eating frogs as a metaphor for tasks, taking on the worst part first. People for whom this idea rings true choose the most difficult, ill-defined, or disliked project as the task they first undertake, attempting to get it off their list and be done with it. When thinking about all they must do, they look for this extreme without considering quick wins, alternatives, or tasks which could mitigate the effort it will take to eat those frogs. Doing the most difficult thing first makes progress and the rest of the list is easier and faster to do, so this preference is not necessarily problematic. When the most difficult thing is too difficult, it will lead to feeling stuck and unproductive. Individuals with a decision bias to *eat the frog* may be inclined to seek a coach to support their productivity.

The ability to get things done is often talent-related; making sure the right things get done requires complementary talents. The role of the coach is not to direct the client to undertake an easier or more difficult task, but to support clients' intentionality in exploring alternative paths so they follow their most effective or efficient way forward.

Goals, subgoals, and timelines

Productivity inherently focuses on goals and often the effort to pursue them; shift focus to envisioning completion. What is the hoped-for result? What is different because of the accomplishment? When is it expected to be realized? This questioning may be applied to many items, as part of the evaluation process, or to an item selected as the goal. When a satisfactory goal is identified and these questions can be answered with clarity, the subgoals and timelines can then be backward planned. To do this, divide the end goal into subgoals with deadlines that support completion by the expected date.

Table 6.1 The Busyness Inventory provides a process to address general productivity needs. Debrief includes exploring talent-focused strategies to address needs and barriers relevant to *important* and *engaging* tasks. Created by the author.

Busyness Inventory → Priorities

All I Do: Activity, Task, Project, Habit, Routine	Why this	This is Important	This is Engaging	For this I usually feel 1-5 scale Dread (1) to Enthusiasm (5)			Schedule items with high *important* and *engaging* values as priorities		
				Starting	Doing	Completing	Best time	Frequency	Ritualize
This	Describe	Scale 1-5 (5=most)	Scale 1-5 (5=most)						

(Continued)

Table 6.1 (Continued)

Busyness Inventory → Priorities

All I Do: Activity, Task, Project, Habit, Routine	Why this	This is Important	This is Engaging	For this I usually feel 1-5 scale Dread (1) to Enthusiasm (5)			Schedule items with high *important* and *engaging* values as priorities		
This	Describe	Scale 1-5 (5=most)	Scale 1-5 (5=most)	Starting	Doing	Completing	Best time	Frequency	Ritualize

Highlight items requiring further analysis or reflection   *items that contribute to your goals by Perception Coaching®   Page___ of___

Subgoals

Pursuit of stretch goals often requires several skills, steps, and processes; parse them into the smallest achievable parts to make progress more visible. Ask, *what is the first thing that must be done?* Alternatively, if there is a clear picture of the final accomplishment, *what is the last step before completion?* When first or last steps are elusive, start brainstorming and recording all the steps and projects, creating a map of all the things that must be done to achieve the goal. Group related items (by project types, resources, or other relevant system), then put them in order, breaking each goal and subgoal into the smallest components possible, as you go. Thus far, the process outlines *what* needs to be accomplished so that the client intentionally focuses productive efforts on the right thing. Next, reinforce *why* these are the right goals, acknowledge possible barriers, and commit to focusing efforts on this worthwhile goal.

> **Delegation**
>
> For an individual producer, the productivity process works best with their preferences in mind. For leaders supporting productivity, consider direct reports and producers' preferences to increase their capacity to perform. Some will be concerned with purpose, others strategic plans, and yet others will be happy to be told what task to complete and when. For successful delegation and directing, it is essential that the individual doing the task engages with the purpose, commitment, and planning to the degree that satisfies their talents and preferences.

Purpose and commitment

Mood and mode are ideas that interact to explain much of engagement. Mode is the way of doing things, which is an obvious contributor to productivity. Mood is emotional, often low in intensity and short in duration, and strangely enough, greatly influences productivity. If the mode related to productively engaging in a task is unknown (*I don't know what they want me to do*), a negative or apprehensive mood regarding the task will likely be triggered; mood becomes a barrier to engagement, and in turn productivity.

As discussed in previous sections, emotions are notifications which require attention; in the case of productivity, one's mood likely indicates an attitude or need that once identified and addressed, will improve their ability to engage and be productive.

Committing to the purpose of goals is embedded in setting them, during the process of reviewing needs and opportunities focused on selecting the right things to do. An opportunity to refine and align goals with values and natural preferences explicitly reinforces goals and creates a productive mood. After processing several potential goals, selecting one, defining the goal to clarify expectations, and breaking it into manageable subgoals, one may lose sight of the initial hope behind the goal. Revisiting the hope or purpose creates a double-check to ensure the subsequent goal did not get off track as it was clarified. Begin with a reminder of the event or need that prompted the goal. Then establish an understanding of the effort the goal requires.

Recognizing needs and anticipating effort increases the robustness of goal commitment. Questions such as *What talents will support your efforts? What resources are at your disposal? Where might you find collaborators or contributors to help with the work?* provide opportunities to see a path forward. Alternatively, *what might be most difficult in this proposed timeline? Which items do you imagine might cause procrastination? What must you learn?* question types clarify needs and prepare for obstacles. Watch for preferences to surface regarding interests, time, energy, and best strategies for focus and engagement. This analysis supports resilience to combat internal barriers that arise in implementation. When a challenging goal is set and one anticipates the barriers, they can prepare and are ready to face it when the barrier appears. This is useful to inform the planning process.

Tracy struggled to get to the gym, even though they had an event coming up for which they needed training. The barrier they encountered before coaching was ill-defined and they felt they were being lazy. Once they acknowledged their reason for reluctance – the best time to exercise was only available because they held that space for sleep – they were able to plan to overcome it. Tracy set a goal of going to the gym every day before work, for the next three months. Knowing they preferred to sleep in, we spent time talking about strategies that energize them to support their commitment. When that early alarm rang, they re-lived the camaraderie they felt being in the gym with their friends or remembered the feeling of fulfillment they had starting work with a workout already completed. On any given day, one or more planned, productive thoughts provided the energy for them to roll out of bed, effectively removing the anticipated barrier. There came a point when the planned thoughts were losing their edge and it was again becoming difficult, so other motivating thoughts were added, and they were able to recount the progress that each day contributed to their overall wellness goal and the affirming comments people made about their dedication to their plan.

Tracy's internal conflict was managed with motivating, energizing thoughts for the three-month period they trained. The strategy was not designed to support a lifestyle change, but effectively supported their time-bound goal; the inconvenience of an early morning routine was temporary, and these thoughts made it more manageable.

I want support for my three-month exercise plan

When a client has a clear goal, remember their autonomy. One could argue that individuals benefit from a lifelong fitness regimen, and that would be an even better goal. Be mindful that goal assignment is not the role of the coach; coach biases are set aside in favor of focusing on the client's intentions.

This caveat is important because individuals come to coaching with a variety of goals and needs and coaches are there to support their efforts. The client is best qualified to judge intentions or alter expectations regarding their goals.

The commitment phase supports clients to process how they will find time and energy to be productive by being mindful of their hopes and preferences. The tensions explored in the commitment phase are often internal and preferential. Once a major tension is removed, a new one may appear. This is the nature of true challenges; they have multiple sticking points or barriers to address. Once commitment is established, the next phase is to plan how to best accomplish the tasks with preferences and talents in mind.

Plan the path and start the journey

Goal setting in the process above included commitments, subgoals, and even timelines. A next step is action planning. The qualitative differences between the tasks and goals listed in a to-do list or inventory must be considered in planning. Some tasks, once added to a day's schedule, are a "gimme" which is to say they happen with little effort or fanfare. They may be included on a checklist or as a calendar task, and once one has a nudge, or reminder, these items are easily done. Other items require strategic thinking, effective timing, research, or otherwise have complexity which planning supports. It is the complex goals with possible complications which we will now address.

Goal quick start plan

1. **What does progress look like?**

    Identify subgoals: time, quantity, or other progress.
    Describe situation or project when complete.

2. **What resources facilitate progress?**

    What materials are required?
    What would be nice?
    How will time be allocated?
    Which talents will contribute and how?

3. **Take action!**

    What needs to happen first?
    Do it with next steps in mind.

A quick start plan is useful when a goal is well-defined and will be carried out independently. It supports the main points of planning; progress is clear, resources are considered, and first steps are taken.

Resources and time management

Once a goal or project is evaluated as worthwhile, explore questions which support finding the right resources, scheduling not only sufficient time, but at the best times, and create a foundation for meaningful progress. This requires pragmatic evaluation. What parts of productivity are easy and flow? What are the pinch points in productivity? What resources support the pursuit of this worthwhile goal? Keep these questions in mind as you select the strategies and approaches to accomplish the goal.

Steps and processes

A plan is an educated guess, a hypothesis, a theory for how something complex or difficult will be accomplished. Often plans and procedures are considered synonymous; this creates issues when something unexpected is introduced to the situation. Plans become procedures when they work consistently in given situations. A powerful question about a plan is, "Does this work for you?"

Establishing procedures that are easy to implement and follow is an undertaking which creates clear performance expectations and a means to support them. When a consistently working procedure exists, behavioral task analysis is used to capture the actions involved in carrying out the steps. On an assembly line, repetitive behaviors are used to increase efficiency; there is little room or reason for changing the behavior. If the process has been analyzed sufficiently, even the exceptions become routine, such as disposing of parts that do not fit as designed. In this environment, when trained procedures are followed, the satisfactory work should be reflected in feedback. Creating procedures for routine tasks creates consistent performance; clients benefit from considering which of their responsibilities might be made more efficient with behavioral task analysis.

Knowing where preferences lead, whether it be planning, doing, or more generally managing productivity, supports focus on the right talents at the right time and optimizes the effects of efforts. Clients' talents and natural dispositions contribute to how they generally succeed. When client success is elusive, work with them to identify where productivity breaks down; investigate the following areas of productivity and explore alternative approaches in the area or step for which challenge exists.

Bias box

Approach

The best approach when entering situations or starting a new endeavor is to think about possibilities and limitations before taking action.

Understanding one's natural patterns of approaches benefits sense of self and supports access to other perspectives. One's first responses to a need or opportunity indicate their natural dispositions for navigating the world; when successful, these talents are reinforced and when used intentionally, become strengths. Additionally, one's attention likely shows preference for people or things when applying these talents.

Relating: Direct and facilitate – this includes managing or coordinating the moving parts and is often at the hub of communication. Related behavior and thinking talents include being adept at sensing and being able to create connections, relationships, and systems. Starting a project by consulting an expert or inventorying materials which may be useful may indicate relating as a preferred approach.

Thinking: Research and plan – this is where the moving parts are identified and understood, and the path is set; it is the cognitive part of any endeavor. Thinking includes talents related to means for gathering information, reasoning, and logic, as well as identifying optimal paths and approaches when pursuing goals. Considering options and best paths, or the biased statement introducing approaches, indicate that thinking may be a preferred approach to projects or work.

Doing: Act and resolve issues – this is when the plan is implemented, the part of a project when behaviors create clearly visible progress. *Doing* talents focus on acting on a plan, and inherently include commitment, as well as motivation, and problem-solving abilities. *Let's get started, what is the first step,* or *tell me what you want me to do* are phrases which indicate a preference for doing.

Talent development focuses on applying preferred approaches appropriately and includes intentionally practicing and improving related talents. Talents are how we do, think, and relate. Weaknesses are described as overused and misused talents. Things we don't naturally do are not weaknesses, they are merely *not our way of doing, thinking, or relating*. With this perspective, when a talent becomes a weakness and is not useful, it is most productive to lean on or develop other natural approaches that can serve the purpose more effectively.

Self-assess

Explore your preferences for pursuing goals and contributing to projects. For each pair mark the strength of your preference between the two anchors; the center is neutral, indicating no preference.

Relating ---- 3 ---- 2 ---- 1 ---- 0 ---- 1 ---- 2 ---- 3 ---- **Thinking**
Relating ---- 3 ---- 2 ---- 1 ---- 0 ---- 1 ---- 2 ---- 3 ---- **Doing**
Doing ---- 3 ---- 2 ---- 1 ---- 0 ---- 1 ---- 2 ---- 3 ---- **Thinking**

Note the order and strength of your preferences.

Reflect and discuss

Consider the purpose, values, and benefits of the three approaches:

1. Describe circumstance or content for which each approach is especially suited:

    - Directing or facilitating actions or materials
    - Researching or planning
    - Taking action or problem solving

2. Holistically, most tasks and goals require all approaches. How might you use your preferred approaches to accomplish the parts which are less preferred?
3. Commitment supports starting, working through challenges, and achieving goals. Describe how commitment may look in each approach.
4. Would you adapt any of these approaches or add others?
5. How does this content contribute to your coaching perspective?

Individual preferences impact how things get done, even when routine tasks and procedures are the focus of productivity. Managing emails can be seen as behavioral in nature; broadly, there are two steps for each message: the message is read, a response is written as appropriate, the next email is processed. While one individual may have a procedure to answer emails at a given time or times every day, another individual may find it difficult to implement such a procedure and plans to complete their email tasks when they have time or find it necessary. Though email communication appears to be a straightforward, procedural task, there exist intervening cognitive factors that add complexity for many individuals.

For example, if one receives 40 emails a day, the time to respond to each is likely variable. The morning's email will contain some reminders; a procedure may be in place to capture deadlines, scheduled meetings, and other time-relevant information. There may be diverse inquiries, which may take extra time to consider and respond; a procedure may be in place to prioritize these by immediacy and importance. There may be planning or work which requires back and forth communication, which also benefits from a procedure to keep up with and capture progress and respond in a timely manner.

Many communications do not readily fit in useful categories labeled by email users. Which brings us to the cognitive aspect of the email management task, which requires reasoning, specifically about categories or groups, for the purpose of efficient processing. Not all individuals are talented in this way of reasoning. Cognitive task analysis complements behavioral task analysis for procedures when behaviors do not explain significant portions of performance variability. Reasoning skills are captured in cognitive task analysis, as well as contingency planning, decision points, even fluently grouping numbers for mental calculation, alphabetizing, and other types of thinking which vary in abstraction and utilize knowledge acquisition and retrieval.

Imagine email management as a microcosm of the multitude of tasks one undertakes, and we can begin to see how individual differences impact productivity. Some individuals are prone to plan for the usual with the attitude that having clear procedures for regular tasks is efficient. Other individuals tend to plan for the exception, seeing more exceptions than similarities in their regular tasks. These perceptual differences impact how they do things; each group invests cognitive power differently. Who may be more efficient at keeping their inbox at zero? Who may take extra time to read a lengthy email to respond appropriately? Responses to these questions are not mutually exclusive by group; though when time is limited, and emails are a primary communication tool, quantity and quality likely compete for focus when performing the task.

Rich discussions stem from exploration of mundane daily routines, such as email management; look for themes regarding how your client processes routine procedures and the disruptions to their planned processes. When working with clients who encounter challenges with routines, consider task analyses, both behavioral and cognitive, to determine where support and efforts matter most.

Align steps and natural ways of doing

Task analyses describe procedures. When barriers arise, or proactively when planning, consider preferences for factors such as immediacy, responding, anticipating, and performing. Individuals may have preferences which guide them; naming them and recognizing the relevance of performance preferences supports efforts. Much like the area of well-being, clients can leverage their preferences to improve outcomes in productivity. Ask questions to clarify task-specific preferences when the task is relevant to a goal or challenge.

Another aspect of processes is their phases or stages. Look at the stages related to productivity to determine how preferences and which talents are at work. The planning stage is often comprised of research and thinking and includes discussions centered around the mission, best way forward, resources required, and possible barriers. The next phase is the implementation of the plan; starting the project is action oriented. This requires motivated energy to get things moving and, depending on the project, a unique combination of skills, talents, and strategies are drawn upon to make things happen. The third phase is the continuation of the plan; a steadfast energy and working consistently are the hallmarks of the middle of a project. Finally, there are the actions required for completing a project. This is often accompanied by a sense of accomplishment, and also some inhibition regarding what is next. Inquire to discover which stages are especially energizing and important.

These broad stages often include intervals of challenge, monotony, and disengagement as well as excitement, improvement, and intensity. Ask clients, "Which of these do you experience most often in projects? For what types of tasks does this change?"

Targeted efforts strategy

Goals and efforts are complementary partners; each is more meaningful when paired with the other. When natural inclinations are to act, effort is the focus. On the other hand, when one's disposition centers on thinking about the possible future, the goal is clear. Often, these approaches are not equally accessible or preferred for individuals.

Goal: Put your goal in the center of three concentric circles. It is the focus of all efforts.

Accelerators: Accelerators are added to the outer ring. What resources will support progress toward the primary goal? The strategies and strengths you will aim at the goal are especially useful. Accelerators are nouns (people, places, things, ideas) and include talents, material resources, as well as people who are supportive.

Effort: Surround your goal with efforts. Look at the accelerators to plan your efforts (verbs, actions you will take toward you goal). If time management is something that increases your progress, it is an accelerator. How you implement an action related to time management is your effort; perhaps you will invest in creating a schedule to find dedicated time for goal work. You may find you need to develop skills or strategies to support progress. Related efforts for people talented in research may be to focus study on best practices or recent developments in the field or area of the goal.

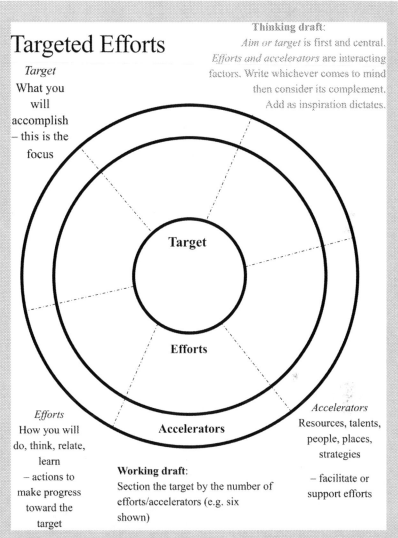

Targeted Efforts

Thinking draft:
Aim or target is first and central.
Efforts and accelerators are interacting
factors. Write whichever comes to mind
then consider its complement.
Add as inspiration dictates.

Target
What you
will
accomplish
– this is the
focus

Target

Efforts

Accelerators

Efforts
How you will
do, think, relate,
learn
– actions to
make progress
toward the
target

Working draft:
Section the target by the number of
efforts/accelerators (e.g. six
shown)

Accelerators
Resources, talents,
people, places,
strategies

– facilitate or
support efforts

Figure 6.1 Targeted Efforts provides a touchpoint to support the power-ful interaction between goal and effort. The model includes accelerators as a power source for efforts; accelerators name the resources, strategies, talents, and partners that support progress toward the goal. Illustration by the author.

Priorities and expectations

Clear expectations support focused efforts. It is important to describe the state that indicates the goal is met or project is done; this may include quality, quantity, time, or other relevant factors. Clarity around how progress is measured supports subgoals and progress checks; progress may be described using quantity or quality expectations.

Clear, well-defined goals support effective planning. Performance addresses how things are done, including processes and competencies. Clear performance criteria are useful to provide feedback and develop skills necessary to accomplish tasks and surpass expectations. Discuss the expectations related to completing the task. Is it an endeavor without an optimized procedure, requiring a creative path or solution? Are there best practices or industry processes that must be followed? Is it a complex project which has both clear procedures and room for optimization or improvement? Each of these types of projects potentially require different skills and cognitive abilities.

Four phases of decisions

Processes provide support for everyday demands and tasks. Some decisions are choices, and others are open-ended, requiring a search for alternatives before a decision is made. Use the following four-step process to intentionally improve decision quality and support effective implementation for making complex decisions.

- Awareness of opportunity to decide, or sense a problem

  What indicates that options are available and should be considered?
  Act: Clarify the opportunity

- Engage in identifying a variety of options to provide decision alternatives

  How and where might the range and diversity of options be increased?
  Act: Research and brainstorm

- Engage in identifying optimal paths to simplify the decision and commit to action

  What factors should be considered essential to a solution?
  Act: Evaluate impact of alternatives; include ease of implementation and quality of solution

- Determine actions, predict barriers, implement

  How will essential factors remain the priority? What is Plan B? Might Plans C and D be needed?
  Act: Implement the decision and face challenges; include progress monitoring

Coaching practices

How it gets done

Start with awareness: *How do your talents contribute to getting things done?*

Aware: Task analyses (behavioral and cognitive)
What behaviors and competencies are required to do the task?
What thinking and decisions are required to do the task?
Debrief: *Are you clear regarding what it takes to do the task? Do you have the skills needed?*

Engaged: Using skills and strategies
How do you create efficiencies when working?
How do you improve performance?
Debrief: *What is needed and what is nice?* Creating a vision with phases or a continuum of successes clarifies goals and supports resource management. Progress partners, journaling, and other strategies support progress. *How do you support continued progress?*

Empowered: Barriers and competing priorities
Where may barriers arise and how can you respond?
How will you navigate other tasks and allocate time, attention, resources, and efforts?
Debrief: *What talents can you call upon to monitor progress and adjust the plan?* Complex and long-range planning cannot account for all factors. Environmental, personal, and other forces create needs to adjust even the most thorough plans.

Reflect and discuss

1. When may each of these questions be useful:

   a. Are you more talented at seeing patterns or handling anomalies?
   b. Do you like to meet challenges or prepare for likely obstacles?
   c. Do you work better under pressure?
   d. Does responding to numerous demands drain your energy?
   e. Do you do best when you can make plan a, b, and c?
   f. What type of work do you enjoy?

2. The questions above are not open. What follow-up questions might you use for each?

Predictable progress

Implementation should mean progress; ensuring that is the case requires fore-thought and adapting when progress slows or stops.

Fluency and adapting

Self-efficacy is essential to productivity; confidence in one's thorough under-standing of the plan will get them to their goal. Discussions or thinking should include focus on skills and talents applicable for understanding the relation-ships among planned processes and in-the-moment decisions. Decisions and processes for creating the plan result in knowing the parts backward and for-ward. When one doesn't feel they have the skills to manage their project, they will hit a wall. If they avoid opportunities to independently adapt their plan, they will not develop requisite problem-solving skills and will flounder when facing barriers. In the face of competing priorities, resource and time manage-ment decisions may need to be made and plans adapted. Long-range plans often have a middle slump, where action fatigue sets in, making progress feel difficult and slow.

The ability to call upon strategies to increase energy and adjust planned approaches will bolster efforts when productivity is difficult. It is benefi-cial to consider the tasks to be done and consider ways you have success-fully completed them in the past. What is needed to make progress: focus, energy, space, materials, or time? Complete the productivity formula (see Figure 6.2) proactively and revisit when there is a barrier to progress or progress slows.

Empowered to navigate challenges

Everyone who pushes to excel faces barriers to their success. Managing resources and time may include unanticipated barriers due to external forces. Additionally, external forces can make one feel powerless or controlled. This brings us back to self-efficacy with regards to carrying out the plan. Plans change to accommodate new information, resources dwindle, and competing demands interfere with timelines; these are only a few circumstances which can derail progress. When productivity is stopped or slowed too much, step back to identify the bottleneck or sticking point. Are the possible tensions task or resource based? Are there strategies or skills that can be developed to reduce the required effort or put the project back on track?

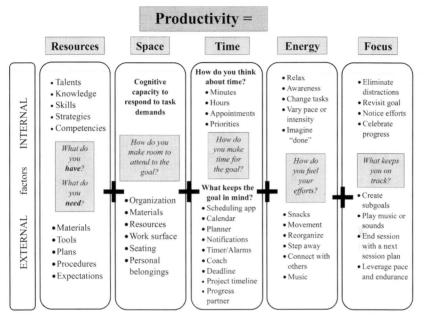

Figure 6.2 The productivity formula is summarized, and samples of the five factors that contribute to productivity are included; note that each factor has both internal and external aspects. Created by the author.

Knowledge, competencies, and tasks

Expectations were briefly discussed in planning. In implementation expectations must be clear and measured using quality, quantity, time-based, or other metrics. It is difficult to strive for and achieve success if one doesn't know what progress looks like or how it can be measured. To support progress for complex or long-range projects, create intermediate measurable expectations.

Develop clarity around requisite knowledge and skills for a given task as the first step to address issues of productivity, including when the quality of work does not meet expectations. Task analyses may need to be two-fold. All tasks likely have behavioral aspects which include actions which must be performed to complete the task. If there are varying levels of precision which improve with practice, include a scale with the optimal level specified. The second aspect is cognitive; cognitive skills can and should be considered as they contribute to effective task performance. Cognitive aspects of tasks include note-taking, various communications, decisions, judgments, analyses, summarizing, and other thinking skills. Include the complexity of task-related thinking and required level of cognition from simple to higher order thinking, as part of task analysis. When task expectations or requirements are clear, clients can effectively aim their talents and efforts to meet their expectations.

Progress, barriers, and resilience

Individuals can have trouble seeing progress, especially in the midst of a long-term project. Accomplishments may be slow, there may be frustrations with unforeseen barriers, fatigue may set in.

Reflecting on progress is one strategy to energize efforts. Whether or not subgoals were in place at the start, consider mapping them by reflecting on accomplishments, challenges overcome, and learning which has occurred thus far in the project.

Realizing the talents or preferences that have been useful or underused and taking fresh aim may also provide energy to sustain progress or overcome barriers.

Coaching practices

Sticking to goals

Start with awareness: *How do your talents contribute to decisions?*

Aware: Many things require attention; some things are worthy of attention
What are you having trouble doing?
Review your list/inventory of projects and tasks and note which you:

- *struggle to engage with (is this a "must do"?)*
- *struggle to find time for (is this a "want to do"?)*
- *are doing (how do you both find time and feel engaged?)*

Debrief: *Star items which are most engaging.* Discuss motivation, talents, and purpose related to engagement. Capturing this is especially valuable over time; revisit it to add items and mark completed and abandoned items to uncover themes, show progress, and highlight talents and needs.

Engaged: Selecting the right steps and metrics adds immense value to plans
What is important to do to make progress?
What is time dependent?
Debrief: *Which subgoal is... most relevant... impactful... must come first... an easy win?* This may be used for the next step in a meaningful path to productivity, providing opportunity and reinforcement for productive behaviors.

Empowered: Renew commitment with better approaches
How will you use your talents that naturally align with the plan?
Which talents support making decisions explicitly?
At what point must you shift your natural approach to use different talents?
How does your plan support your efforts?
Debrief: *How do your preferences support accomplishing the goal and adapting as needed?* The reevaluation of steps and talents may result in reorganization, elimination, refining task labels or descriptive phrases, and otherwise clarifying goal items.

When one aspect of productive behavior or thinking is causing tension, stepping back and seeking alternatives may provide relief or a better way to proceed. Even our natural preferences can be overused, or stretched too far. Consider other talents that may support the activity that is a struggle. Reach out for help from someone who has fresh energy, or step away to do something else for a period of time to return with renewed energy. Changing perspectives from doing to thinking or vice-versa can also create a path forward. Consider what your needs are and which talents may provide you a bridge to productivity.

Navigating challenges can be equally involved with internal conflict and external forces. By starting with the client's perspective and what is in their control, they can better reengage with their project or task to feel more productive. Though it may feel like a detour, finding ways around external sources of frustration is often productive in itself, and moves the project forward. Planned paths are not a procedure, but a map to ensure one is true to the direction they choose. When detours happen, the plan is in mind so that it may resume once the barrier or challenge is sufficiently mitigated. A good plan supports resilience when this is the approach.

Coaching practices

Inspired to act

Individuals often struggle to find motivation to act when their talents and task are not aligned, their energy is low, or the task is not a priority or important to them.

Aware: Analyze recent and past successes
What are you always motivated to do?
How have you found motivation in the past?

Engaged: Look to talent, purpose, and time for inspiration
How can your talents help?
How is this important?
When is the best time to do this?
How will you find energy to act?

Empowered: What changes after you act?
What does your action impact?
Who benefits from your action?

Development, feedback, and growth

Challenges and mistakes provide opportunities to learn and grow. When this attitude is functioning, resilience is empowered. Development around task competencies includes both knowledge and application, and growth requires practice to achieve near perfect execution every time.

Productive feedback is seen in the quality of interaction while doing things, whether it is self-talk or elicited from others. Leading with positive intent becomes difficult when interactions are transactional, you have expectations of them, and there is a real or implied hierarchy of power. In such cases, clear communication is essential, especially for any expectations involved. To lead with positive intent we ask *how are you?* When focus is on expectations or feedback ask: *what do you need to meet this expectation?* Agreeing on expectations supports leading with positive intent. Additionally, both parties benefit from the fulfillment of the expectations, and authentic feedback is provided to support fulfillment. The attitude that everyone is doing their best is key.

Working with others

Working in teams and other group arrangements adds factors which, when compared to being an individual contributor, have potential to improve solutions, and enhance performance. Similar and complementary preferences enhance productivity and may lead to tensions.

Collaborative relationships and teams

Collaboration for productivity increases wisdom for the work. Navigating diverse viewpoints and approaches takes time and effort which results in happier team members, bolstering the quality of the work.

For the greatest productive effect in establishing the collaboration, norm setting and well-being considerations include sharing task-relevant preferences, talents, and needs. This serves multiple important purposes.

Task–talent alignment

The idioms many hands make light work and the right person for the job provide insight which support efficient and effective results. Team development which focuses on understanding each other's work and social preferences increases the ability of members to communicate effectively. Related preferences may include process talents like strategy or implementation; understanding who thrives doing these things supports the team's efforts. There may be individuals who work best alone, some who prefer working alongside others. The purpose of teamwork is to leverage the talents of its members to achieve what one cannot accomplish alone; their work does not necessarily require proximity. Cooperation and communication hold a team together.

Communication

Clear communication in a team or organization is facilitated by understanding member communication preferences. Some members wonder how decisions were made while others only want to know how the decision impacts them or their work; therefore transparent communication is in the eye of the beholder. Communication systems in a productive team include places where progress of tasks, resource allocation, and requests, as well as barriers that arise, are shared. Weekly or daily meetings, electronic organizers and schedulers, a central hub, and other systems meet the needs of diverse communication preferences.

Leading a group or organization

Leading for productivity starts with clear expectations. When expectations are clear, leaders can effectively support those who strive to meet them. Directing and delegating create an atmosphere of productivity where individuals work with challenge and support aligned to their preferences.

Leaders who are producers

Individuals who are elevated to manage others because of their talents as contributors may struggle with letting go of their proven methods and appreciating the approaches preferred by others. *My way or the highway* is a leadership approach which severely limits an organization; without diverse perspectives or means of doing business stagnation will occur.

Suspending judgment and becoming curious are first and foremost for the leader in this situation. Once preferences are understood, the leader's expertise can inform ways to support another approach. Leadership development with a focus on translating the success of the leader to expertise which supports different approaches, preferences, and aspects of productivity will create a culture where stakeholders and everyone in the organization interact authentically to maximize results.

Reflect and discuss

1. If a client is struggling to do quality work, on what part of productivity might you focus?
2. Where might you focus a client whose direct reports are not producing quality work?
3. Which tools or strategies related to productivity will you add to your toolbox?
4. Refer to Appendix Table A.1; select a client profile.

   a. What questions might you pose regarding expectations and productivity?
   b. What indicates an opportunity to explore missions and goals?

Innovation and opportunity-hypotheses development

7

Goals: Unique solutions, processes, systems, and resources which improve quality of life

Efforts: Opportunity-hypotheses development; understand needs, optimize solutions, support implementation

Opportunity-hypotheses development is... in these sections we will provide ideas on awareness, then engagement and empowerment. Innovation is born when a connection between knowledge and previously unconnected needs or opportunities is recognized; it can be the result of unsought insight or perseverance and determination. Regardless of the means which bring about an innovative idea, opportunities abound to support the development and realization of innovation.

There has got to be a better way!

A client came to the appointment at their wits end; their board is impatient, and the client experiences the same stress every quarter. Quarterly reports from department heads are due before the board meeting, and each inevitably is rushed to get the data from the past quarter, create and share their report, so it can then be reviewed and summarizing by the client, before presenting the information to the board. The board meeting is always the second Wednesday of the

DOI: 10.4324/9781003332770-10

month and members want time to read the summary before the meeting. When first proposed this timeline seemed tight, but manageable. Now, two years later, quarter end is dreaded by the client, as well as their department heads, their direct reports, and some board members.

Coaching provides perspective in situations like this by questioning expectations and assumptions to uncover unnecessary or arbitrary parameters. This begins the client's journey to create improved or new processes which make life better.

Innovation, invention, creative solutions... there are numerous ways to express this concept. Perception Coaching® addresses the means of change, be it a shift from the status quo or creation of something new. The goal of innovation is to create something which brings hope for the future.

Curiosity and seeking opportunities

Suspending judgment

People have evolved to be curious about their surroundings so that they can identify threats; without another goal, this remains the default. Generate curious, productive questions to suspend judgment and create opportunities to sense new perspectives, make connections between previously unrelated ideas, and pursue alternatives. Curiosity is a characteristic that presents itself in many forms and intensities. Developing curiosity increases learning potential. When curiosity is primed, questions replace judgments and conclusions, creating space to learn.

Regarding the client with quarterly report pressures, the feeling of failure every quarter was suspended to create space to think. Once they stepped back, they recognized the stress was self-imposed by the plan set when they first started their position. There are opportunities to change both processes and timelines which contribute unnecessary stress.

Be curious to understand bold statements

Especially fertile ground for sowing curiosity surprisingly exists in bold statements such as, "I know a lot about an individual as soon as we meet."

Confident, intuitive individuals often appear to lack curiosity, and may not be very curious because they naturally draw quick conclusions. Exploring confidence and learning may cause tension around identity and a barrier to curiosity may be discovered. Sentiments such as *I am known for my ability to learn* may cause dissonance when a perception that *questions infer ignorance* are both held true. Explore the perceived contradiction. When there are challenges to generating authentic questions, navigate tensions between the benefits of being confident and having a curious attitude. It may be that when the client works to clarify preferences, talents, and sense of self, they learn in other ways and their confidence is a strength. Not all clients benefit from reflection and digging into preferences and will put a behavior into practice; they may try out questioning strategies to experience asking questions and evaluating the results. *What else* and *tell me more* are common phrases used in coaching and are valuable strategies for clients who seek probing questions. Developing an attitude of curiosity forges paths to perceptive shifts.

To support practicing curiosity, clients select question stems relevant to their topic of interest; is interest drawn to *when, what, how, who,* or *where*? Curious questions reinforce the idea that more information exists and encourage exploration. An individual who is curious suspends conclusions and increases their ability to include diverse perspectives and optimize with agility.

Coaching practices

Increase curiosity – overcome overconfidence

Aware: Opportunities for curiosity abound
Warm up: *What ideas, topics, or perspectives intrigue you?*
Main question: When is curiosity your natural approach?

Engaged: Question what you know to sense more
How can you find other ways of interpreting what you know?
How might someone reach a different conclusion?

Empowered: Suspend judgment to develop expertise
What assumptions have been made?
What factors have not been considered?
What if parameters were shifted?

Note: Engaged and empowered level questions may be "homework" to process more deeply between coaching sessions.

Purpose and possibilities

Whether one is setting out to innovate, or merely setting the stage for innovation, focusing on and developing expertise facilitates creating new representations and ways of doing. A key to innovation is developing an optimistic attitude toward change; finding the good in change gives one hope and supports efforts for optimization.

Explore barriers or tensions as these indicate areas ready for change. Ask questions to determine chronic needs or untapped potential to explore opportunities for innovation. Identify pain points to find fertile ground for innovation with potential to improve well-being and quality of life.

Goals: Experience and expertise

When seeking opportunities to innovate, start in areas of expertise and interest to provide an excellent foundation for expansion to developing novel representations, which suggest innovative approaches or solutions. Mental representations associated with concepts are refined with experience. Those concepts for which one holds expertise are robust; expert representations recognize identifying traits as well as a variety of characteristics that though not defining, may also occur. As expertise grows experience creates a network of related ideas, as ideas related to the focus of expertise are mentally connected.

When a client has a mission or vision, they are likely ready and willing to create change in their industry or interest area. Immersion describes how passions occupy the mind and drive activities; to support innovation use intentional reflection. This powerful strategy is helpful for generating new representations for conceptual knowledge, understanding complexity, and managing tensions when complications arise. Clients can explore these in discussion or, as between-session work, record a list of daily activities to intentionally focus reflection on aspects of life they wish to investigate.

Ways of doing

Systems and processes are often considered the tried and true paths to well-being or productivity. Limited access and scarcity of resources may indicate needs. It is surprising that there is much waste in some places while need exists in others. Innovators in areas of conservation, particularly food and energy, often explore the question *How can one optimize the use of existing resources?*

Cultivate creativity

Creating space for innovation requires intentional separation of processes, particularly when generating possibilities; in creativity all brainstormed ideas are valued and contribute to the process of finding novelty. Creativity revisits existing ideas to build, redefine, and combine to invent something better. To innovate, one becomes a collector of interesting things, starting with areas of expertise. Explore perspectives regarding concepts including –related as well as unrelated and interesting niche ideas. The brainstorming phase requires one to suspend judgment to create an unbiased index of ideas, unbiased in the sense that all ideas therein are worthy, have potential, and may hold at least part of a unique solution. When organized as a mind map, there is even more power to find interesting links by connecting ideas that were not naturally associated. The mind map, or idea index, is a holding space for thoughts, phrases, and ideas with potential and may evolve to be part of the integration space strategy described later.

Coaching practices

Creativity – generating ideas

Aware: Ideas to fuel creative work are everywhere
Warm up: *What is a new thing you have tried or researched?*
Main question: *How do you notice and keep track of interesting things?*

Engaged: Passion gives creativity a venue
About what do you have deep knowledge?
What interests or causes do you pursue with passion?

Empowered: Creativity benefits from iterations over time
When do you take time to create?
What creative habits or rituals do you have?

Note: Engaged and empowered level questions may be "homework" to process more deeply between coaching sessions.

Seek options and alternatives

Individuals who pursue experiences to learn and grow increase their resilience, well-being, and expertise; new knowledge also increases the possibility of opportunities to innovate. Look for:

• Existing challenges or stagnancies
• Related topics and industries
• Practices across topics and industries

But that's for education and I work in a business. Avoid limiting exploration to practices in your context. Consider the original context of an idea as proof of concept, or a starting point. To innovate, hypothesize and experiment to test the validity in other contexts.

Seeking prompts new perspective: how others may sense the experience, feel about the experience, and interact while in the experience, or observing the event. Seeking supports deeper understanding by approaching the familiar in a new way; this enhances the ability to sense new facets of complex and abstract subjects.

The seeking process is a creative one, which may stretch some pragmatists. For scientific or strategic thinkers, it is productive to frame seeking as *hypothesizing*. Seeking suggestion: one thinks of someone they know who experiences the world differently than them. How might they feel about the experience? Or imagine an "opposite" view; if the client enjoyed the event, what may be the experience of someone who did not enjoy it? What might they sense, and how might they feel experiencing the event?

Identifying what is important provides a reference point when making decisions, plans, and commitments. Having an inventory or index of all factors is beneficial for prioritizing, identifying gaps, overlaps, ambiguity, and identifying opportunities and preferences. Clients assemble lists when seeking to identify interest areas, challenges, stressors, learning topics, or potential goals to pursue for the coaching engagement. Sources for alternatives include topic relevant assessments, brainstorming, card sorts, and other means of research.

Bias box

Next big thing

Curiosity is the most valuable ability for those who hope to find novel solutions.

Invention is born out of three ideas which are similar, yet each serves a different purpose. When one is curious, there is room for exploration and questioning the current situation. Creativity allows one to combine unrelated ideas to see a new product or way of doing. Innovation is the action which puts imagination in the realm of possibility. Individuals working on the cutting edge of technology, social sciences, and many other industries may have some or all of these abilities and work from their preferences as they work on the next big thing in their fields.

Curiosity: Seeking and questioning behaviors, where one identifies potential and opportunities by wondering what has been tried, what is the current state, and what is possible, relate to curiosity. In terms of problem-solving heuristics, curiosity is useful for seeing and understanding the problem.

Flexible thinkers are often curious. Support curiosity with questioning skills, research methods, as well as opportunities to challenge certainty or the status quo.

Creativity: Generating unique ideas, representations, and perspectives relies on creativity. Creativity leads to intuitive problem solving, creatively combining knowledge through a process of incubation and insight.

Fluency of ideas is a hallmark of creativity. Support creativity by supporting the ability to brainstorm, finding unique ways to interact with existing knowledge or items, and developing expertise from which to create.

Innovation: Often curiosity and creativity result in innovation, a new system of thinking, doing, or relating. Innovators are often pragmatic, elaborating and verifying to implement or build the ideas borne of curiosity and creativity.

Change and originality indicate innovation. Support innovation by creating a culture of productive risk taking; physical and psychological safety must be sensed. Reinforce that failure and mistakes are opportunities to learn and grow in ways that lead to discovery.

Self-assess

What ability are you drawn to when change is needed, or you are looking for a new approach? For each pair mark the strength of your preference between the two anchors; the center is neutral, indicating no preference.

Curiosity ---- 3 ---- 2 ---- 1 ---- 0 ---- 1 ---- 2 ---- 3 ---- **Creativity**
Curiosity ---- 3 ---- 2 ---- 1 ---- 0 ---- 1 ---- 2 ---- 3 ---- **Innovation**
Innovation ---- 3 ---- 2 ---- 1 ---- 0 ---- 1 ---- 2 ---- 3 ---- **Creativity**

Note the order and strength of your preferences.

Reflect and discuss

Consider the purpose, values, and benefits of the three abilities:

1. Describe circumstance or content for which each is most useful:
   - Curiosity
   - Creativity
   - Innovation
2. The levels of these ideas appear to be sequential, with curiosity being first. Describe a situation in which following this sequence may not be useful.
3. How does this content contribute to your coaching perspective?

Next, we will explore the evaluation and prioritization process, which occurs away from brainstorming, and is initiated by insight or a persistent pursuit regarding a specific idea or set of ideas. This in turn may lead to creating hypotheses for performing experiments.

Hypotheses and experiments

The beauty of innovation is that it can start with a small step. Consider the goal of the innovation and create a plan that encourages productive risk with a plan for proof of concept or a partial shift.

Hypothesize: this productive risk supports well-being or social-emotional development… or cognitive-behavioral development or productivity. Client questions may include, *What makes this risk worthwhile?*

Research and evaluate

This phase is where ideas are subjected to critical curiosity to estimate potential. Expertise is further developed, practicality is considered, and impact is predicted. Determining the viability of worthwhile ideas requires time, energy, and strategic efforts. New ideas are riddled with unknowns; *what if* thinking is useful to develop expertise and direct exploration to effectively approximate potential benefits, consequences, and collateral implications.

Deepen expertise by researching related practices, as well as evolving practices and theories. When your research is focused on potential it can easily lead you off course with multiple new connecting ideas. It is wise to have your idea index available as a holding place for discoveries as you go.

Estimate impact. What is the benefit of this idea? Does it make something easier? Is it a new approach with potential? Are there ways to expand the idea to improve potential?

Consider and judge practicality

Revisit the previous section's productivity strategies as means to explore and understand relevant goals, resources, and possible paths to make an intriguingly innovative idea something one can adopt as a new way of doing or thinking or that can be realized as an object, service, or other kind of product. How might the idea be developed? What may be the cost of change the idea causes? What development and implementation phases make sense to create substantial impact and simultaneously lessen the burden of change?

When evaluating ideas, you may discover not all have a clear path forward to realization. It is worth archiving ideas that do not make the practicality cut; other innovations may make the idea more viable in the future.

Leading for innovation

Organizational innovation happens in an environment which values diversity, curiosity, and productive risk. When all members of the organization have optimism that their work contributes to the success of the organization, their efforts are appreciated, and they are valued for their authenticity, innovation has room to flourish.

Live with purpose and vision

Individuals dedicated to a calling, career, or passion know why they get up in the morning. They sense how or where they fit in their communities or even the world. For some, this develops naturally and is clear. Their talents, interests, experiences, and opportunities have pointed them to their purpose. Others seek their purpose, exploring possibilities and pursuing diverse interests, open to opportunities which resonate. Often time and changes in circumstances cause one to reflect and reconsider career, calling, or passion, bringing about a new phase in life.

Some may wonder why this is not part of the first section of topics. As a subtopic, living with purpose and vision is arguably more impactful and connected than its parent topic, innovation. Purpose alone is an immense topic, with infinite possibilities when presented as a client goal.

It is last, however, because well-being and productivity include topics which likely include the key to identifying one's purpose and developing clear vision. Developing well-being and productivity strategies supports one to become a leader in their own life, and if preferences align, the lives of others. Individuals strive for satisfaction, contentment, accomplishment, and contribution; pursuing goals related to one's needs is indicative of life lived with purpose and vision. As goals evolve and pursuit continues, self-actualization and even philanthropy become the target for intentional effort.

Things are better and will continue to improve because we do the work. When individuals are a part of something greater than themselves, they aim their efforts with purpose and direction. The potential or observed impact their efforts have on a common or greater goal is a source of optimism.

A leader who supports this improves retention, engagement, and the success of others.

We can innovate to create a world where everyone has what they need. When one imagines a small change that would impact an aspect of life, or pictures an ideal world, they use this vision as motivation, a driving force to make progress. Vision does not have to be an otherworldly gift; when encouraged it grows.

Separate ideation and evaluation

Executives who enable system-wide innovation recognize leaders exist at every level of their organization. Ideas are seeds of optimism which are protected, not evaluated and rejected to be lost to future consideration. Systems that support innovation treat all ideas like valuable resources, gathering and storing them for later access. Idea creation is rewarded, and there is a process to save, connect, and revisit ideas which functions much like in an individual's long-term memory. Having an integration space is effective for an individual, team, or organization.

> Individual integration spaces take many forms, physical and cognitive, as individual preferences dictate; when the space exists for group use, access and clarity must be considered, including the preferences of all involved.

Integration space strategy

Make space to consider new ideas and other perspectives without judgment or conclusions. When clients are creative, they often start a session by sharing all the ideas they have incubating in their minds. When a stream of consciousness seems to be the client focus, listen for repeating themes. Record phrases and ideas that come forth with energy. The index of ideas is only part of what one archives. Ideas which cause cognitive dissonance are also stored here, ambiguously existing with established knowledge. With these disparate bits of knowledge, tensions, barriers, and challenges are stored. The integration space is mental, a journal, electronic whiteboard, or poster which contains the fodder for reflection, explorations, and means by which ideas connect, and productivity and well-being are exhibited and improved. Opportunities to grow can be cultivated here, as well as hopes and dreams, lessons learned, and stubborn questions.

Long-term memory strategies leveraging the attention power of goals expand the mind's definition of relevant to capture creativity-enhancing knowledge. Attention is naturally drawn to unique features in the environment, primarily to determine if they pose a risk. The constant scanning of the environment to check for risks naturally limits what is processed. Things judged as nonthreatening or irrelevant are regularly ignored or dismissed. This evolutionary development is an implicit default for most minds.

Suspending judgment and living with ambiguity both require interrupting implicit processes in favor of explicit thinking. Intentionally dismissing less information creates opportunities for seeing more perspectives on ourselves, others, and the world around us.

Integration space strategies

1. Determine area(s) of interest

   a. Set intention, mission, or vision
   b. Seek ideas, facts, and observations
   c. Seek evidence for relevance

2. Develop expertise with intention

   a. Learn
   b. Practice
   c. Collaborate

3. Hold ambiguity regarding experiences and observations

   a. Suspend judgment

      i. Hold ideas
      ii. Explicitly process to remember original form (avoid loss and mislearning)

   b. Resist labels, categorizing, and overlay (generalizing based on one trait)

      i. Assume multi-dimensionality
      ii. Seek aspects of complexity

c. Actively process cognitive dissonance
   i. Explicitly clarify the observations and knowledge which are "at odds"
   ii. Consider the sources, biases, and intent of the new and existing information
   iii. What if all are true, or untrue; under what circumstances may that be?
4. Be open to alternatives
   a. Brainstorming
   b. Cross discipline practices
   c. Combining disparate ideas
   d. Perception check
   e. Perspectives of others

In an organization, curiosity and ideation provide energy and support improvement. When navigating life with others, asking questions and proposing new perspectives includes inherent risks; innovation depends on these behaviors and approaches. Ideas and curiosity, once discouraged, are difficult to nurture. This is due to the implications for psychological and emotional safety.

New teachers fresh out of college and teacher training come to the profession full of idealistic plans including things they remembered fondly as learners, techniques that would have made their past learning better, as well as ideas from best practice research explored in teacher education. Student teachers and new teaching staff are mentored by experienced teachers; when the experience gap is bridged, it often has a negative impact on optimism. For example, a new teacher enthusiastically mentions, "I am going to set a time for discovery learning, to help students develop curiosity and become more autonomous learners." Their more experienced colleague responds, "I tried that, and we have to get through so much content there was no way to do that too, it takes too much time, it is not possible." This may be enough to quash enthusiasm; after multiple interactions like this with a variety of other teachers, the new teacher will feel dismissed, devalued, and will hesitate to share ideas in the future. The new teacher has discovered this is not a culture which can support their ideas. The veteran teachers are bridging the experience gap by relating anecdotal information, intending to support the new teacher, and inadvertently protecting the status quo. This happens across industries and organizations including healthcare, engineering, leadership, manufacturing, and sales. As an alternative in the teaching example, mentors may suggest that implementing discovery learning may have to wait, as processes and techniques for core learning should first be mastered. Then, to engage the new teacher's ideation, how, when, and other curious questions are asked to support developing a way to implement discovery learning. Outright judgment or dismissal of ideas is counterproductive, hurting the individual and organization.

Brainstorming sessions focus on a question or topic and often include a rule that all ideas are accepted. Even impractical or seemingly disparate ideas contribute to and benefit the exploration of the topic. In an innovative environment, all ideas are stored and can be revisited; a system where ideation is not immediately met with judgment is beneficial to innovation. Determining when and how all or specific ideas are revisited and pursued are separate processes which include judgment around needs, resources, and practicality.

Evaluation and development

Much like in an individual's life in an organization, challenges and barriers indicate opportunities for innovation. This is where ideas are processed to determine which to develop to address organizational needs.

Due to rural needs and globalization, the informal integration spaces of many organizations likely include ideas regarding the abilities of employees to interact with each other as well as with customers at a distance. Before 2020 diverse industries started limited implementation of virtual processes to meet employee and market demands. Virtual marketing and learning were developed to deliver niche content to reach more consumers and students. Few industries, however, were prepared to change entire systems to accommodate greater proportions of people using these options. In March 2020 the pandemic prompted these ideas and experiments to evolve and spread quickly, making innovators in this area wildly successful.

As the urgency of the pandemic recedes, life has changed for many. The practices put in place during the pandemic are regularly subjected to reevaluation. The benefits and drawbacks are now in stark relief, as distancing and in-person practices are seen by many as equally viable options. Preferences and competencies are now center stage as organizations and individuals navigate their virtual and in-person environments, determining what works and what must change.

Commitment and pursuit

Innovation is often a result of the synthesis of well-being and productivity, the benefit of which is greater than the two parts alone. Time marches on and individuals choose to make progress as they continue to learn, adapt, and try new things. Dedication to purpose and vision supports overcoming distractions and barriers. Hope and vision describe an ideal and provide energy to start working toward the goal state. Even with hope and dedication, in the process there will be a time when energy wanes and determination and perseverance are required to continue to make progress.

To pursue innovation, as an individual or leading an organization, it is beneficial to monitor well-being when stamina and endurance are needed. Mostly, is one engaged and empowered by the project or mission's hope and vision? Strategies for productivity also support innovative missions; clear expectations and efforts that align with preferences facilitate continued progress. Commitment is tested when competing priorities arise, barriers appear, or purpose is lost. Innovation is the epitome of a stretch goal. The strategies for well-being and productivity support innovation and innovative solutions support each of these.

In 2023 many work and home environments retain aspects of the innovation created to facilitate productivity and well-being in 2020. For some the purpose of the innovation has faded, for others it is still present. More than other times in recent history, individual preferences and awareness seem to be more actively weighed against organizational needs and best fit relationships are sought by all parties.

Frumar et al. (2023) shared Gallup's research in which hybrid work arrangements are preferred by 61% of respondents, and that 53% of those who do remote-capable work have hybrid arrangements. The technological systems for distance interactions and work adapted much more quickly than the people systems. Strategies for communication, support, management, and other competencies did not become established in a systematic way. Many businesses and organizations sense the benefits of and demand for virtual work options; those organizations are still innovating with a focus on how to build relationships among hybrid and virtual stakeholders, as well as effectively supporting and developing employees who do not share a location.

Change is difficult

As is often the case when change occurs, some organizations and individuals are abandoning the innovations which grew out of the pandemic and were used out of necessity. The reasoning for this is risk aversion and a view that innovation is chaotic.

It comes with too many problems or *There is too much to learn* indicates the individual or organization is overwhelmed by the shortcomings of the innovation or related unknowns. That is not to say the previous system was working, only that there are new tensions associated with the innovation. An organization may have this perspective if it lacks competence to problem solve or face new challenges.

The changes were temporary or *It was not broken* are reasons which means the existing system was working for the individual or organization and innovation is an unnecessary risk. This may indicate a stagnant organization, one without the capacity to adapt to future demands or changes that happen around it.

Capacity and competence

Capacity captures the present limits of an individual's or group's ability to perform. *Competence* includes the fluency of skills, strategies, and knowledge which are applied to performance. Capacity and competence can be developed; the development of one will influence the other.

Leadership development is often focused on capacity building. Individuals use their talents and skills according to preferences which results in uneven application of abilities. Attitudes and beliefs can begin to explain why transfer of knowledge and abilities is limited. Development is facilitated by examining how and when competencies are applied. Example areas to explore include how abilities are used as an individual, to improve the organization, and in creating an environment which supports development. Leaders grow capacity when they increase their ability to apply their competencies to the areas needed by their organization targeting goals to produce, perform, or lead.

Reflect and discuss

1. In what circumstances may increasing curiosity support a client's progress?
2. Why may a client seek to develop their creative ability?
3. How can one ensure systems to support ideation and an integration space are separate from evaluation and development?
4. How does innovation relate to other topics of development:
    a. Well-being
    b. Productivity
    c. Others?
5. Refer to Appendix Table A.1; select a client profile.
    a. What questions might you pose regarding innovation?
    b. What indicates an opportunity to explore curiosity and creativity?

Implications of Perception Coaching

8

The mission and purpose of Perception Coaching® is to improve performance through the lens of perspective. We each filter our state of being, thoughts and actions, and our related gifts and needs using our preferences, experiences, and expertise. Developing an accurate sense of self provides meaningful insights to support meeting challenges, pursuing goals, and living a happy fulfilling life. Three attitudes of perceptive people are: authenticity is appreciated, autonomy is empowering, and differences are valued. Perception Coaching® clients are often reminded:

Authentic behavior builds lasting connections

Your preferences are important aspects of your authentic self. Make space to share your authentic self. When being yourself feels unwelcome, consider alternative approaches that are also you. Find ways to access aspects of safety, comfort, and purpose that support you.

Preferences indicate the mode that works best

Your natural ways of doing are powerful. Develop them to face challenges and overcome barriers. Find ways to identify your gifts and core values to develop your sense of self.

Remember autonomy to process and manage mood

Your emotions are information. Reactions to others, situations, and events are reflections of you and your perspective. When you feel someone brings you joy or unhappiness, note your perceptions of them or the situation. Find ways to manage expectations to manage negative feelings.

There is more to the world; be curious

A rich life of experience, learning, and insight exists in every individual. Become curious about possibilities and the limitations your preferences create

DOI: 10.4324/9781003332770-11

to sense more. Find ways to understand and appreciate alternate approaches and perspectives.

Productive attitudes create courage

Challenges are opportunities to make things better. When tensions or issues interfere with well-being or productivity, effort is required to face them. Find ways to reframe the barrier by imagining a future without it, then create goals to make it possible.

Bias box

Goals and development

Start client conversations with a question about their talents for insights into goals, learning, and needs.

A client's purpose for seeking out a coach is often complex. Coaching conversations navigate content to understand goals and preferences; progress regarding the goal often occurs while exploring effective models of support and development. How do you prefer to navigate client needs?

Talents: Natural approaches, practiced skills, and preferred methods. Identifying and developing talents is the most effective means to bridge gaps, mitigate tensions, and improve performance.

What have you tried? What do you think may work?

Target: The goal or hoped-for outcome. The broad topics of well-being, productivity, and innovation may be the development focus, or the target may be role relevant skill acquisition.

What do you hope to accomplish? What is your current challenge?

Support: Examples are development and progress monitoring. Determining the best form of support is a process, like finding the best actions to take. Individual needs vary greatly.

How do you want me to help? Are you working on a project or developing a routine?

Often clients come to coaching for help, without a specific goal, knowing their talents, or understanding the support a coach can provide. A coach with a clear understanding of their own preferences can support a client's experience exploring the opportunities coaching can uncover.

Self-assess

Consider your focus when coaching; which aspect do you enjoy exploring with clients? For each pair mark the strength of your preference between the two anchors; the center is neutral, indicating no preference.

Talents ---- 3 ---- 2 ---- 1 ---- 0 ---- 1 ---- 2 ---- 3 ---- **Target**
Talents ---- 3 ---- 2 ---- 1 ---- 0 ---- 1 ---- 2 ---- 3 ---- **Support**
Support ---- 3 ---- 2 ---- 1 ---- 0 ---- 1 ---- 2 ---- 3 ---- **Target**

Note the order and strength of your preferences.

Reflect and discuss

Consider the purpose, values, and benefits of the three aspects:

1. Describe circumstance or client need for which each approach is especially suited:

    -   Exploring and developing talents
    -   Identifying and pursuing goals
    -   Trying different support options

2. Progress is starting, working through challenges and achieving goals. Describe how progress may look in each approach.
3. Holistically, most tasks and goals require all aspects of coaching. How might you use your preferred approaches to accomplish the parts which are less preferred? Are there other aspects you value?
4. How does this content contribute to your coaching perspective?

Conclusion

Individuals are researchers and each life is an exceptionally valid experiment ($N = 1$), the implications of which are enriched by learning through sharing results with others. Perceptions are the result of each experiment which includes several studies, with a sample of one. Reliability is the goal; to increase reliability, other researchers are considered and valued, new parameters are set, and the experiment continues.

Perception Coaching® brings the implicit processes of the experiment to the forefront, supporting client efforts to improve their data analysis and intentionally make progress as they craft new experimental studies to improve well-being, productivity, and innovation while sensing more in their environment.

The greatest opportunity is found in sharing. The implications of Perception Coaching® are many, and more will likely originate from readers who sense potential or alternatives outside of the author's experience.

There is always another perspective and strategy, especially in performance coaching. As you consider the Perception Coaching® model, make it your own: does your perspective on goals align with the topics of well-being, productivity, and innovation, or do you sense a topic that falls outside of these? What is the goal and how might awareness, engagement, and empowerment be developed? How may understanding capacity and preferences for learning contribute to exploring the topic?

Appendix

Client intake forms

Client intake forms are valuable tools which can serve many purposes. Initially, getting basic client information may be the purpose. The questions asked on such a form are likely perceived by the client in many ways. Therefore, a secondary purpose may be to introduce the client to the coaching practice. Finally, well considered questions and prompts lend themselves to repetition, providing a measure for client progress.

Form rationale

Though not visible in Table A.1, when the form is opened, participants first see the company logo and title: *What I do well*. A powerful title on an intake form sets the tone for coaching interactions; *What I do well* indicates sessions are client focused and optimistic.

The questions are intended to provide insight regarding client perceptions of talent and goals. Initial responses serve as a baseline; as talent development and goal pursuit progress, the form can be administered again. This serves an essential function as the effects of coaching can be difficult to measure. Subsequent results are expected to include ideas discussed in coaching, including growing expertise in talents and clarity in goals.

As you consider creating an intake form, ensure that it is informative, easy to manage, and convenient for clients.

Table A.1 is the output of an electronic intake form. Each line includes authentic responses to the prompts to create the sample client profile. Created by the author.

What is your greatest talent? or What do you do well?	What talents do you use everyday?	What are your greatest accomplishments?	What are your greatest goals?	What is your role or profession?
I can bring a calmness to other people's anxiety	I listen a lot and share information	I finished my bachelors degree and have been improving my public speaking skills	To help people as much as I can	Coach/Speaker
Accumulating resources/ information and sharing with others, encouraging others	Information seeking; educating others, advocate, empathy, compassion	Recognized by co-workers as someone they can come to for information, listening ear, encouragement; ultrarunning (finished several 100 mile races in addition to other distances); close relationships with a small core group	Continue thriving in my job and in my personal life, finding balance between the two	RN
Using creativity for enjoyment as well as to help solve problems	People skills, problem solving, teaching youth, and creativity	Working in a profession that helps others overcome challenges and achieve improved functioning	Having work life balance, achieving expertise in my field of work, and finding fulfillment and purpose through my work	Pediatric occupational therapist
My empathy for others. I listen to people and I care about them	I help my co workers, adapt quickly to change, remain calm under pressure, brainstorm on the spot during difficult situations	Becoming what I've wanted to be since I was a little girl - a nurse. Also running a half marathon (twice)	Caring for others as long as I can and becoming a mentor to future healthcare professionals	Registered nurse

(Continued)

Table A.1 (Continued)

What is your greatest talent? or What do you do well?	What talents do you use everyday?	What are your greatest accomplishments?	What are your greatest goals?	What is your role or profession?
Organizing, creating, teaching	Organizing, empathy, advocacy	Education (getting my doctorate), running two marathons, living my life after surviving cancer feels like an accomplishment every day	This question is hard for me to answer. It has been difficult for me to set goals after having/ surviving cancer and treatment. My goal was to graduate my doctoral program and pass my board exam. I did that. Now I'm not really sure what my goals are. I've been having a hard time setting goals	Psychiatric nurse practitioner
Sensitive to other people and caring, helping them feel better mentally and physically	Working with clients. Helping them relax and relieving soreness and pain	Helping people feel better every day, relax	Continue to always help others and improve others' quality of life	Massage therapist
Reflection	Kindness, seeking to understand, attention to detail	Becoming independent	To live life by my terms	Teacher
Have fun	Listen	Having children	To stay healthy - avoid disease	Personal trainer
Trying new things	Teaching, helping	My dog	Family and mental health	Teaching and understand about insurance

(Continued)

Table A.1 (Continued)

What is your greatest talent? or What do you do well?	What talents do you use everyday?	What are your greatest accomplishments?	What are your greatest goals?	What is your role or profession?
Organization, perseverance, detail oriented	Organization	Getting into pharmacy school, completing my BA	Complete my PharmD and get a fulfilling job	Student/ pharmacy intern
Listening skills and empathy	People skills, empathy, organization	Work - helping kids with psychological issues, finding resources. Family - working part-time to maintain lots of family time	Continue helping people, stay connected with close ties to family, friends	Patient service assistant scheduler/ med secretary
Communicating difficult topics, educating people, providing compassionate support	Communication, empathy, listening skills	Learning a second language, graduating with my bachelor's, volunteering with those in need	Get into graduate school, learn another language, improve mental health and heal past trauma	Genetic counseling assistant
Extremely driven	Attention to detail, people skills (extrovert)	Graduating pharmacy school, attending/presenting research at conferences	Helping patients - being told 'yes' to their needs/desires to improve their health	Pharmacist
Think and get things done	Researching, observation, and connecting ideas	Being an entrepreneur	Increase success so that I can share the benefits	Coach
Systems thinking	Organization, communication, analysis	Promotion to director position	Develop a legacy system	Healthcare administration

(Continued)

Table A.1 (Continued)

What is your greatest talent? or What do you do well?	What talents do you use everyday?	What are your greatest accomplishments?	What are your greatest goals?	What is your role or profession?
Creativity and languages	Communication, curiosity, and relationship building	Landed dream job in top tech company	To create a business which leverages my diverse interests	Software engineer
Relationship building	Communication, responsibility, creative problem solving	Promoted to team lead	Work with an ethical start up	Customer service
Teaching and learning	Communication, problem solving, researching	Earned MEd	Make education more accessible and valuable	Educator

Bibliography

Abelson, R. P., Aronson, E., McGuire, W. J., Newcomb, T. M., Rosenberg, M. J., & Tannenbaum, P. H. (Eds.) (1968). *Theories of Cognitive Consistency: A Sourcebook.* Chicago: Rand McNally and Co.

Abrantes, A. C. M., Passos, A. M., Pina e Cunha, M., & Miner, A. S. (2020). Managing the unforeseen when time is scarce: How temporal personality and team improvised adaptation can foster team performance. *Group Dynamics: Theory, Research, and Practice, 24*(1), 42–58. https://doi.org/10.1037/gdn0000113

Achtypi, E., Ashby, N. J. S., Brown, G. D. A., Walasek, L., & Yechiam, E. (2021). The endowment effect and beliefs about the market. *Decision, 8*(1), 16–35. https://doi.org/10.1037/dec0000143

Ackley, D. (2016). Emotional intelligence: A practical review of models, measures, and applications. *Consulting Psychology Journal: Practice and Research, 68*(4), 269–286. https://doi.org/10.1037/cpb0000070

Ackoff, R. L. (1978). *The Art of Problem Solving, Accompanied by Ackoff's Fables.* New York: John Wiley & Sons, Inc.

Adair, J. (2007). *Decision Making & Problem Solving Strategies.* Philadelphia: Kogan Page Limited.

Adams, J. S. (1968). A framework for the study of modes of resolving inconsistency. In Abelson, R. P., Aronson, E., McGuire, W. J., Newcomb, T. M., Rosenberg, M. J., & Tannenbaum, P. H. (Eds.) *Theories of Cognitive Consistency: A Sourcebook,* 655–660. Chicago: Rand McNally and Co.

Agmon, G., Loewenstein, Y., & Grodzinsky, Y. (2022). Negative sentences exhibit a sustained effect in delayed verification tasks. *Journal of Experimental Psychology: Learning, Memory, and Cognition, 48*(1), 122–141. https://doi.org/10.1037/xlm0001059

Alarcon, G. M., Capiola, A., Lee, M. A., & Jessup, S. (2022). The effects of trustworthiness manipulations on trustworthiness perceptions and risk-taking behaviors. *Decision, 9*(4), 388–406.

Altizer, C. C., Ferrell, B. T., & Natale, A. N. (2021). Mindfulness and personality: More natural for some than others and how it matters. *Consulting Psychology Journal: Practice and Research, 73*(1), 51–64. https://doi.org/10.1037/cpb0000189

Annis, J., Dubé, C., & Malmberg, K. J. (2018). A Bayesian approach to discriminating between biased responding and sequential dependencies in binary choice data. *Decision*, *5*(1), 16–41. https://doi.org/10.1037/dec0000060

Aronson, E. (1968). Dissonance theory: Progress and problems. In Abelson, R. P., Aronson, E., McGuire, W. J, Newcomb, T. M., Rosenberg, M. J., & Tannenbaum, P. H. (Eds.) *Theories of Cognitive Consistency: A Sourcebook*, 5–27. Chicago: Rand McNally and Co.

Attali, Y., Budescu, D., & Arieli-Attali, M. (2020). An item response approach to calibration of confidence judgments. *Decision*, *7*(1), 1–19. https://doi.org/10.1037/dec0000111

Bachkirova, T. (2016). The self of the coach: Conceptualization, issues, and opportunities for practitioner development. *Consulting Psychology Journal: Practice and Research*, *68*(2), 143–156. https://doi.org/10.1037/cpb0000055

Bailey, P. E., Ebner, N. C., Moustafa, A. A., Phillips, J. R., Leon, T., & Weidemann, G. (2021). The weight of advice in older age. *Decision*, *8*(2), 123–132. https://doi.org/10.1037/dec0000138

Bandura, C. T., Kavussanu, M., & Ong, C. W. (2019). Authentic leadership and task cohesion: The mediating role of trust and team sacrifice. *Group Dynamics: Theory, Research, and Practice*, *23*(3–4), 185–194. https://doi.org/10.1037/gdn0000105

Barkan, R., Ayal, S., & Ariely, D. (2016). Revisiting constructed preferences: Extrapolating preferences from relevant reminders. *Decision*, *3*(4), 281–294. https://doi.org/10.1037/dec0000051

Barlow, H. B. (1961). Possible principles underlying the transformations of sensory messages. In Rosenblith, W. (Ed.) *Sensory Communication*. Cambridge, MA: MIT Press.

Batson, C. D. (2022). Prosocial motivation: A Lewinian approach. *Motivation Science*, *8*(1), 1–10. https://doi.org/10.1037/mot0000217

Beersma, B., Greer, L. L., Dalenberg, S., & De Dreu, C. K. W. (2016). Need for structure as asset and liability in dynamic team decision-making. *Group Dynamics: Theory, Research, and Practice*, *20*(1), 16–33. https://doi.org/10.1037/gdn0000037

Behrendt, P., Mühlberger, C., Göritz, A. S., & Jonas, E. (2021). Relationship, purpose, and change – An integrative model of coach behavior. *Consulting Psychology Journal: Practice and Research*, *73*(2), 103–121. https://doi.org/10.1037/cpb0000197

Bennett, S. T., & Steyvers, M. (2022). Leveraging metacognitive ability to improve crowd accuracy via impossible questions. *Decision*, *9*(1), 60–73. https://doi.org/10.1037/dec0000165

Berger, D. E., Pezdek, K., & Banks, W. P. (1987). *Applications of Cognitive Psychology: Problem Solving, Education, and Computing*. Hillsdale, NJ: Lawrence Erlbaum Associates, Publishers.

Berkman, E. T. (2018). The neuroscience of goals and behavior change. *Consulting Psychology Journal: Practice and Research*, *70*(1), 28–44. https://doi.org/10.1037/cpb0000094

Berlyne, D. E. (1968). The motivational significance of collative variables and conflict. *Theories of Cognitive Consistency: A Sourcebook*, 257–266. Chicago: Rand McNally and Co.

Bhatia, S., & Golman, R. (2019). Attention and reference dependence. *Decision*, *6*(2), 145–170. https://doi.org/10.1037/dec0000094

Bhatia, S., & Richie, R. (2022). Transformer networks of human conceptual knowledge. *Psychological Review*. Advance online publication. https://doi.org/10.1037/rev0000319

Bhui, R. (2019). Falling behind: Time and expectations-based reference dependence. *Decision*, *6*(3), 287–303. https://doi.org/10.1037/dec0000102

Bhui, R., & Gershman, S. J. (2020) Paradoxical effects of persuasive messages. *Decision*, *7*(4), 239–258. https://doi.org/10.1037/dec0000123

Bleichrodt, H., L'Haridon, O., & Van Ass, D. (2018). The risk attitudes of professional athletes: Optimism and success are related. *Decision, 5*(2), 95–118. https://doi.org/10.1037/dec0000067

Bothe, D. R. (2002). *Reducing Process Variation: Using the DOTSTAR Problem-Solving Strategy Volumes 1 & 2.* Cedarburg, WI: Landmark Publishing Co.

Bourne, A., & Whybrow, A. (2019). Using psychometrics in coaching. In Palmer, S., & Whybrow, A. (Eds.) *Handbook of Coaching Psychology: A Guide for Practitioners* (2nd edn), 512–526. New York: Routledge.

Boyatzis, R. E. (2016). Commentary on Ackley (2016): Updates on the ESCI as the behavioral level of emotional intelligence. *Consulting Psychology Journal: Practice and Research, 68*(4), 287–293. https://doi.org/10.1037/cpb0000074

Boyatzis, R. E., Goleman, D., Dhar, U., & Osiri, J. K. (2021). Thrive and survive: Assessing personal sustainability. *Consulting Psychology Journal: Practice and Research, 73*(1), 27–50. https://doi.org/10.1037/cpb0000193

Boyatzis, R. E., & Jack, A. I. (2018). The neuroscience of coaching. *Consulting Psychology Journal: Practice and Research, 70*(1), 11–27. https://doi.org/10.1037/cpb0000095

Brainerd, C. J., Chang, M., & Bialer, D. M. (2021). Emotional ambiguity and memory. *Journal of Experimental Psychology: General, 150*(8), 1476–1499. https://doi.org/10.1037/xge0001011

Bremnes, H. S., Szymanik, J., & Baggio, G. (2022). Computational complexity explains neural differences in quantifier verification. *Cognition, 223*, 1–18. https://doi.org/10.1016/j.cognition.2022.105013

Brown, M. I., Prewett, M. S., & Grossenbacher, M. A. (2020). Distancing ourselves from geographic dispersion: An examination of perceived virtuality in teams. *Group Dynamics: Theory, Research, and Practice, 24*(3), 168–185. https://doi.org/10.1037/gdn0000120

Brown, S. I., & Walter, M. I. (1990). *The Art of Problem Posing* (2nd edn). Hillsdale, NJ: Lawrence Erlbaum Associates, Publishers.

Campbell, J. I. D. (Ed.) (2005). *Handbook of Mathematical Cognition.* New York: Psychology Press.

Cavanaugh, C., & Green, K. (2020). Training faculty search committees to improve racial and ethnic diversity in hiring. *Consulting Psychology Journal: Practice and Research, 72*(4), 263–274. https://doi.org/10.1037/cpb0000167

Choi, H.-S., & Yoon, Y.-J. (2018). Collectivistic values and an independent mindset jointly promote group creativity: Further evidence for a synergy model. *Group Dynamics: Theory, Research, and Practice, 22*(4), 236–248. https://doi.org/10.1037/gdn0000093

Chou, E. Y., & Phillips, K. W. (2022). Unpacking the Black box: How inter- and intra-team forces motivate team rationality. *Decision, 9*(3), 250–262. https://doi.org/10.1037/dec0000178

Clifton, D. O., & Nelson, P. (2010). *Soar with Your Strengths: A Simple Yet Revolutionary Philosophy of Business and Management.* New York: Bantam Books.

Clifton, J., & Harter, J. (2021). *Wellbeing at Work: How to Build Resilient and Thriving Teams.* New York: Gallup Press.

Cohen, D., & Teodorescu, K. (2022). On the effect of perceived patterns in decisions from sampling. *Decision, 9*(1), 21–42. https://doi.org/10.1037/dec0000159

Colby, K. M. (1968). A programmable theory of cognition and affect in individual personal belief systems. *Theories of Cognitive Consistency: A Sourcebook,* 520–525. Chicago: Rand McNally and Co.

Collins, M. A., & Amabile, T. M. (1999). Motivation and creativity. In Sternberg, R. J. (Ed.) *Handbook of Creativity*, 297–312. New York: Cambridge University Press.

Coultas, C. W., & Salas, E. (2015). Identity construction in coaching: Schemas, information processing, and goal commitment. *Consulting Psychology Journal: Practice and Research, 67*(4), 298–325. https://doi.org/10.1037/cpb0000046

Csikszentmihalyi, M. (1997). *Creativity: Flow and the Psychology of Discovery and Invention*. New York: Harper Perennial.

Dagley, G. R., & Gaskin, C. J. (2014). Understanding executive presence: Perspectives of business professionals. *Consulting Psychology Journal: Practice and Research, 66*(3), 197–211. https://doi.org/10.1037/cpb0000011

Dartnell, T. (Ed.) (2002). *An Interaction: Creativity, Cognition, and Knowledge*. Westport, CT: Praeger Publishers.

Davis, A. L., Miller, J. H., & Bhatia, S. (2018). Are preferences for allocating harm rational? *Decision, 5*(4), 287–305. https://doi.org/10.1037/dec0000076

Davis, G. A., & Rimm, S. B. (2004). *Education of the Gifted and Talented* (5th edn). New York: Pearson Education, Inc.

de Haan, E., Grant, A. M., Burger, Y., & Eriksson, P.-O. (2016). A large-scale study of executive and workplace coaching: The relative contributions of relationship, personality match, and self-efficacy. *Consulting Psychology Journal: Practice and Research, 68*(3), 189–207. https://doi.org/10.1037/cpb0000058

de Haan, E., Molyn, J., & Nilsson, V. O. (2020). New findings on the effectiveness of the coaching relationship: Time to think differently about active ingredients? *Consulting Psychology Journal: Practice and Research, 72*(3), 155–167. https://doi.org/10.1037/cpb0000175

de la Malla, C., & López-Moliner, J. (2022). Scene variability biases our decisions, but not our perceptual estimates. *Journal of Experimental Psychology: Human Perception and Performance*. Advance online publication. https://doi.org/10.1037/xhp0001061

De Meuse, K. P. (2017). Learning agility: Its evolution as a psychological construct and its empirical relationship to leader success. *Consulting Psychology Journal: Practice and Research, 69*(4), 267–295. https://doi.org/10.1037/cpb0000100

de Ridder, D., Kroese, F., & Gillebaart, M. (2018). Whatever happened to self-control? A proposal for integrating notions from trait self-control studies into state self-control research. *Motivation Science, 4*(1), 39–49. https://doi.org/10.1037/mot0000062

Debnath, M., Hasanat-E-Rabbi, S., Hamim, O. F., Hoque, M. S., McIlroy, R. C., Plant, K. L., & Stanton, N. A. (2021). An investigation of urban pedestrian behaviour in Bangladesh using the Perceptual Cycle Model. *Safety Science, 138*, Article 105214. https://doi.org/10.1016/j.ssci.2021.105214

Dixon, J. A. (2005). Mathematical problem solving: The roles of exemplar, schema, and relational representations. In Campbell, J. I. D. (Ed.) *Handbook of Mathematical Cognition*, 379–395. New York: Psychology Press.

Dombroski, T. W. (2000). *Creative Problem Solving: The Door to Progress and Change*. Lincoln, NE: toExcel Press.

Dozois, D. J. A. (2021). The importance of social connectedness: From interpersonal schemas in depression to relationship functioning and well-being. *Canadian Psychology/Psychologie canadienne, 62*(2), 174–180. https://doi.org/10.1037/cap0000253

Drapeau, P. (2014). *Sparking Student Creativity: Practical Ways to Promote Innovative Thinking and Problem Solving*. Alexandria, VA: ASCD.

Egan Brad, L. C., Lakshminarayanan, V. R., Jordan, M. R., Phillips, W. C., & Santos, L. R. (2016). The evolution and development of peak-end effects for past and prospective experiences. *Journal of Neuroscience, Psychology, and Economics, 9*(1), 1–13. https://doi.org/10.1037/npe0000048

Eichinger, R. W. (2018). Should we get aboard the brain train? *Consulting Psychology Journal: Practice and Research, 70*(1), 89–94. https://doi.org/10.1037/cpb0000107

Emanuel, A., Katzir, M., & Liberman, N. (2022). Why do people increase effort near a deadline? An opportunity-cost model of goal gradients. *Journal of Experimental Psychology: General, 151*(11), 2910–2926. https://doi.org/10.1037/xge0001218

Ericsson, K. A. (2003). The acquisition of expert performance as problem solving. In Davidson, J. E., & Sternberg, R. J. (Eds.) *The Psychology of Problem Solving*, 31–83. New York: Cambridge University Press.

Feist, G. J. (1999). The influence of personality on artistic and scientific creativity. In Sternberg, R. J. (Ed.) *Handbook of Creativity*, 273–296. New York: Cambridge University Press.

Feldman, D. H. (1999). The development of creativity. In Sternberg, R. J. (Ed.) *Handbook of Creativity*, 169–186. New York: Cambridge University Press.

Filipowicz, A., Valadao, D., Anderson, B., & Danckert, J. (2018). Rejecting outliers: Surprising changes do not always improve belief updating. *Decision, 5*(3), 165–176. https://doi.org/10.1037/dec0000073

Fogler, H. S., & LeBlanc, S. E. (1995). *Strategies for Creative Problem Solving*. Upper Saddle River, NJ: Prentice Hall, Inc.

Forestier, C., de Chanaleilles, M., Boisgontier, M. P., & Chalabaev, A. (2022). From ego depletion to self-control fatigue: A review of criticisms along with new perspectives for the investigation and replication of a multicomponent phenomenon. *Motivation Science, 8*(1), 19–32. https://doi.org/10.1037/mot0000262

Forrest, J., Vogt, J., McDonald, C., Searle, C., & Sakaki, M. (2022). Blind to threat: The presence of temporary goals prevents attention to imminent threat already at early stages of attention allocation. *Motivation Science, 8*(3), 239–251. https://doi.org/10.1037/mot0000261

Frumar, C., Truscott-Smith, A., & Schatz, J. (2023). *How to Make Hybrid Work for Women*. www.gallup.com/workplace/471239/hybrid-work-women.aspx

Galesic, M., Barkoczi, D., & Katsikopoulos, K. (2018). Smaller crowds outperform larger crowds and individuals in realistic task conditions. *Decision, 5*(1), 1–15. https://doi.org/10.1037/dec0000059

Garner, J. T., & Ragland, J. P. (2019). Tabling, discussing, and giving in: Dissent in workgroups. *Group Dynamics: Theory, Research, and Practice, 23*(1), 57–74. https://doi.org/10.1037/gdn0000098

Gavrilova, Y., Donohue, B., Galante, M., & Gavrilova, E. (2019). A controlled examination of motivational strategies: Is it better to motivate by reviewing positive consequences for goal achievement or negative consequences of not accomplishing goals? *Motivation Science, 5*(3), 235–256. https://doi.org/10.1037/mot0000118

Gendolla, G. H. E., Bouzidi, Y. S., Arvaniti, S., Gollwitzer, P. M., & Oettingen, G. (2021). Task choice immunizes against incidental affective influences in volition. *Motivation Science, 7*(3), 229–241. https://doi.org/10.1037/mot0000225

Gershman, S. J. (2019). Uncertainty and exploration. *Decision, 6*(3), 277–286. https://doi.org/10.1037/dec0000101

Gessnitzer, S., Schulte, E.-M., & Kauffeld, S. (2016). "I am going to succeed": The power of self-efficient language in coaching and how coaches can use it. *Consulting Psychology Journal: Practice and Research, 68*(4), 294–312. https://doi.org/10.1037/cpb0000064

Gevers, J. M. P., Rispens, S., & Li, J. (2016). Pacing style diversity and team collaboration: The moderating effects of temporal familiarity and action planning. *Group Dynamics: Theory, Research, and Practice, 20*(2), 78–92. https://doi.org/10.1037/gdn0000049

Ghassemi, M., Wolf, B. M., Bettschart, M., Kreibich, A., Herrmann, M., & Brandstätter, V. (2021). The dynamics of doubt: Short-term fluctuations and predictors of doubts in personal goal pursuit. *Motivation Science, 7*(2), 153–164. https://doi.org/10.1037/mot0000210

Gieseler, K., Loschelder, D. D., Job, V., & Friese, M. (2021). A preregistered test of competing theories to explain ego depletion effects using psychophysiological indicators of mental effort. *Motivation Science, 7*(1), 32–45. https://doi.org/10.1037/mot0000183

Gnilka, P. B., McLaulin, S. E., Ashby, J. S., & Allen, M. C. (2017). Coping resources as mediators of multidimensional perfectionism and burnout. *Consulting Psychology Journal: Practice and Research, 69*(3), 209–222. https://doi.org/10.1037/cpb0000078

Golman, R., & Loewenstein, G. (2018). Information gaps: A theory of preferences regarding the presence and absence of information. *Decision, 5*(3), 143–164. https://doi.org/10.1037/dec0000068

Gøtzsche-Astrup, O. (2018). The bright and dark sides of talent at work: A study of the personalities of talent-development-program participants. *Consulting Psychology Journal: Practice and Research, 70*(2), 167–181. https://doi.org/10.1037/cpb0000105

Grant, A. M. (2017). Solution-focused cognitive-behavioral coaching for sustainable high performance and circumventing stress, fatigue, and burnout. *Consulting Psychology Journal: Practice and Research, 69*(2), 98–111. https://doi.org/10.1037/cpb0000086

Grawitch, M. J., Waldrop, J. S., Erb, K. R., Werth, P. M., & Guarino, S. N. (2017). Productivity loss due to mental- and physical-health decrements: Distinctions in research and practice. *Consulting Psychology Journal: Practice and Research, 69*(2), 112–129. https://doi.org/10.1037/cpb0000089

Green, S., & Palmer, S. (2019). *Positive Psychology Coaching in Practice.* New York: Routledge.

Guan, M., & Lee, M. D. (2018). The effect of goals and environments on human performance in optimal stopping problems. *Decision, 5*(4), 339–361. https://doi.org/10.1037/dec0000081

Guastello, S. J., Correro, A. N. II, & Marra, D. E. (2018). Do emergent leaders experience greater workload? The swallowtail catastrophe model and changes in leadership in an emergency response simulation. *Group Dynamics: Theory, Research, and Practice, 22*(4), 200–222. https://doi.org/10.1037/gdn0000091

Guiney, M. C., Newman, D. S., Øverup, C. S., & Harris, A. (2020). Learning the language of consultation: Quantifying interactions over time. *Consulting Psychology Journal: Practice and Research, 72*(2), 100–118. https://doi.org/10.1037/cpb0000154

Haase, C. M., Singer, T., Silbereisen, R. K., Heckhausen, J., & Wrosch, C. (2021). Well-being as a resource for goal reengagement: Evidence from two longitudinal studies. *Motivation Science, 7*(1), 21–31. https://doi.org/10.1037/mot0000199

Hai-Dong, L., Ya-Juan, Y., & Lu, L. (2022). In the context of COVID-19: The impact of employees' risk perception on work engagement. *Connection Science, 34*(1), 1367–1383. https://doi.org/10.1080/09540091.2022.2071839

Hallett, M. G., & Hoffman, B. (2014). Performing under pressure: Cultivating the peak performance mindset for workplace excellence. *Consulting Psychology Journal: Practice and Research, 66*(3), 212–230. https://doi.org/10.1037/cpb0000009

Hamm, J. M., Perry, R. P., Chipperfield, J. G., Parker, P. C., & Heckhausen, J. (2019). A motivation treatment to enhance goal engagement in online learning environments: Assisting failure-prone college students with low optimism. *Motivation Science, 5*(2), 116–134. https://doi.org/10.1037/mot0000107

Hawkins, G. E., Islam, T., & Marley, A. A. J. (2019). Like it or not, you are using one value representation. *Decision, 6*(3), 237–260. https://doi.org/10.1037/dec0000100

Hawthorne-Madell, D., & Goodman, N. D. (2019). Reasoning about social sources to learn from actions and outcomes. *Decision, 6*(1), 17–60. https://doi.org/10.1037/dec0000088

Hayes, T. L., Oltman, K. A., Kaylor, L. E., & Belgudri, A. (2020). How leaders can become more committed to diversity management. *Consulting Psychology Journal: Practice and Research, 72*(4), 247–262. https://doi.org/10.1037/cpb0000171

Hayes, T. R., & Henderson, J. M. (2021). Looking for semantic similarity: What a vector-space model of semantics can tell us about attention in real-world scenes. *Psychological Science, 32*(8), 1262–1270. https://doi.org/10.1177/0956797621994768

Hayes, W. M., & Wedell, D. H. (2020). Modeling the role of feelings in the Iowa Gambling Task. *Decision, 7*(1), 67–89. https://doi.org/10.1037/dec0000116

Heeren, G., Markett, S., Montag, C., Gibbons, H., & Reuter, M. (2016). Decision conflict and loss aversion – An ERP study. *Journal of Neuroscience, Psychology, and Economics, 9*(1), 50–63. https://doi.org/10.1037/npe0000052

Helman, P., & Veroff, R. (1986). *Intermediate Problem Solving and Data Structures: Walls and Mirrors*. Menlo Park, CA: The Benjamin/Cummings Publishing Company, Inc.

Hennecke, M. (2019). What doesn't kill you…: Means for avoidance goal pursuit are less enjoyable than means for approach goal pursuit. *Motivation Science, 5*(1), 1–13. https://doi.org/10.1037/mot0000104

Hoenig, C. (2000). *The Problem Solving Journey: Your Guide for Making Decisions and Getting Results*. Cambridge, MA: Perseus Publishing.

Hoffmann, J. A., von Helversen, B., & Rieskamp, J. (2019). Testing learning mechanisms of rule-based judgment. *Decision, 6*(4), 305–334. https://doi.org/10.1037/dec0000109

Hoffmann, P., Platow, M. J., Read, E., Mansfield, T., Carron-Arthur, B., & Stanton, M. (2020). Perceived self-in-group prototypicality enhances the benefits of social identification for psychological well-being. *Group Dynamics: Theory, Research, and Practice, 24*(4), 213–226. https://doi.org/10.1037/gdn0000119

Holtz, K., Orengo Castella, V., Zornoza Abad, A., & González-Anta, B. (2020). Virtual team functioning: Modeling the affective and cognitive effects of an emotional management intervention. *Group Dynamics: Theory, Research, and Practice, 24*(3), 153–167. https://doi.org/10.1037/gdn0000141

Hommelhoff, S., Richter, D., Niessen, C., Gerstorf, D., & Heckhausen, J. (2020). Being unengaged at work but still dedicating time and energy: A longitudinal study. *Motivation Science, 6*(4), 368–373. https://doi.org/10.1037/mot0000155

Hoover, J. D., & Healy, A. F. (2019). The bat-and-ball problem: Stronger evidence in support of a conscious error process. *Decision, 6*(4), 369–380. https://doi.org/10.1037/dec0000107

Hotaling, J. M. (2020). Decision field theory-planning: A cognitive model of planning on the fly in multistage decision making. *Decision, 7*(1), 20–42. https://doi.org/10.1037/dec0000113

Hotaling, J. M., & Rieskamp, J. (2019). A quantitative test of computational models of multialternative context effects. *Decision, 6*(3), 201–222. https://doi.org/10.1037/dec0000096

Howansky, K., Dominick, J. K., & Cole, S. (2019). The look of success or failure: Biased self-perceptions serve as informational feedback during goal pursuit. *Motivation Science, 5*(4), 314–325. https://doi.org/10.1037/mot0000121

Huang, Y., Dong, J., He, Y., Hei, Y., Duan, X., Zhang, W., & Yan, H. (2022). Language specificity in the processing of affirmative and negative sentences. *Neuroreport: An International Journal for the Rapid Communication of Research in Neuroscience, 33*(4), 153–162. https://doi.org/10.1097/WNR.0000000000001771

Hull, C. L. (1932). The goal-gradient hypothesis and maze learning. *Psychological Review, 39*(1), 25–43. https://doi.org/10.1037/h0072640

Ianiro, P. M., & Kauffeld, S. (2014). Take care what you bring with you: How coaches' mood and interpersonal behavior affect coaching success. *Consulting Psychology Journal: Practice and Research, 66*(3), 231–257. https://doi.org/10.1037/cpb0000012

IJntema, R. C., Ybema, J. F., Burger, Y. D., & Schaufeli, W. B. (2021). Building resilience resources during organizational change: A longitudinal quasi-experimental field study. *Consulting Psychology Journal: Practice and Research, 73*(4), 302–324. https://doi.org/10.1037/cpb0000218

Jessup, R. K., Busemeyer, J. R., Dimperio, E., Homer, J., & Phillips, A. (2022). Choice is a tricky thing: Integrating sophisticated choice models with learning processes to better account for complex choice behavior. *Decision, 9*(3), 221–249. https://doi.org/10.1037/dec0000171

Jessup, R. K., Ritchie, L. E., & Homer, J. (2020). Hurry up and decide: Empirical tests of the choice overload effect using cognitive process models. *Decision, 7*(2), 137–152. https://doi.org/10.1037/dec0000115

Jonas, E., & Mühlberger, C. (2017). Editorial: Social cognition, motivation, and interaction: How do people respond to threats in social interactions? *Frontiers in Psychology, 8.* https://doi.org/10.3389/fpsyg.2017.01577

Joseph, S., & Bryant-Jefferies, R. (2019). Person-centred coaching psychology. In Palmer, S., & Whybrow, A. (Eds.) *Handbook of Coaching Psychology: A Guide for Practitioners* (2nd edn), 131–143. New York: Routledge.

Kaftan, O. J., & Freund, A. M. (2019). A motivational perspective on academic procrastination: Goal focus affects how students perceive activities while procrastinating. *Motivation Science, 5*(2), 135–156. https://doi.org/10.1037/mot0000110

Kaiser, R. B. (2020). Leading in an unprecedented global crisis: The heightened importance of versatility. *Consulting Psychology Journal: Practice and Research, 72*(3), 135–154. https://doi.org/10.1037/cpb0000186

Kaney, T. (2017). Transitioning into the role of trusted leadership advisor. *Consulting Psychology Journal: Practice and Research, 69*(1), 29–31. https://doi.org/10.1037/cpb0000080

Kaplan, B., & Crockett, W. H. (1968). Developmental analysis of modes of resolution. *Theories of Cognitive Consistency: A Sourcebook*, 661–669. Chicago: Rand McNally and Co.

Kauffman, C., & Hodgetts, W. H. (2016). Model agility: Coaching effectiveness and four perspectives on a case study. *Consulting Psychology Journal: Practice and Research, 68*(2), 157–176. https://doi.org/10.1037/cpb0000062

Kaufman, J. C. (2009). *Creativity 101.* New York: Springer Publishing Company LLC.

Kellen, D. (2022). Behavioral decision research is not a Linda problem: Comment on Regenwetter et al. (2022). *Decision, 9*(2), 112–117. https://doi.org/10.1037/dec0000170

Khademi, M., Schmid Mast, M., & Frauendorfer, D. (2020). From hierarchical to egalitarian: Hierarchy steepness depends on speaking time feedback and task interdependence. *Group Dynamics: Theory, Research, and Practice, 24*(4), 261–275. https://doi.org/10.1037/gdn0000114

Kilburg, R. R. (2016). The development of human expertise: Toward a model for the 21st-century practice of coaching, consulting, and general applied psychology. *Consulting Psychology Journal: Practice and Research*, 68(2), 177–187. https://doi.org/10.1037/cpb0000054

Kilburg, R. R. (2017). Trusted leadership advisor: A commentary on expertise and ethical conundrums. *Consulting Psychology Journal: Practice and Research*, 69(1), 41–46. https://doi.org/10.1037/cpb0000085

Kilpatrick, F. P., & Cantril, H. (1960). Self-anchoring scaling: A measure of individuals' unique reality worlds. *Journal of Individual Psychology*, 16(2), 158.

Kip, A., & Evers, C. (2020). Let go and give in! Self-licensing and the role of competing motivations. *Motivation Science*, 6(4), 359–367. https://doi.org/10.1037/mot0000167

Knight, J. (2016). *Better Conversations: Coaching Ourselves and Each Other to Be More Credible, Caring, and Connected*. Thousand Oaks, CA: Corwin.

Koltko-Rivera, M. E. (2006). Rediscovering the later version of Maslow's Hierarchy of Needs: Self-transcendence and opportunities for theory, research, and unification. *Review of General Psychology*, 10(4), 302–317. https://doi.org/10.1037/1089-2680.10.4.302

Konstantinidis, E., van Ravenzwaaij, D., Güney, Ş., & Newell, B. R. (2020). Now for sure or later with a risk? Modeling risky intertemporal choice as accumulated preference. *Decision*, 7(2), 91–120. https://doi.org/10.1037/dec0000103

Kool, W., & Botvinick, M. (2014). A labor/leisure tradeoff in cognitive control. *Motivation Science*, 1(S), 3–18. https://doi.org/10.1037/2333-8113.1.S.3

Kuntz, J. R. C., Malinen, S., & Näswall, K. (2017). Employee resilience: Directions for resilience development. *Consulting Psychology Journal: Practice and Research*, 69(3), 223–242. https://doi.org/10.1037/cpb0000097

Kvam, P. D., & Pleskac, T. J. (2017). A quantum information architecture for cue-based heuristics. *Decision*, 4(4), 197–233. https://doi.org/10.1037/dec0000070

Lane, D., Simon Kahn, M., & Chapman, L. (2019). Adult learning as an approach to coaching. In Palmer, S., & Whybrow, A. (Eds.) *Handbook of Coaching Psychology: A Guide for Practitioners* (2nd edn), 369–380. New York: Routledge.

Lee, D. G., & Hare, T. A. (2022). Evidence accumulates for individual attributes during value-based decisions. *Decision*. Advance online publication. https://doi.org/10.1037/dec0000190

Lee, D. G., & Holyoak, K. J. (2021). Coherence shifts in attribute evaluations. *Decision*, 8(4), 257–276. https://doi.org/10.1037/dec0000151

Lee, G. C., Platow, M. J., Haslam, S. A., Reicher, S. D., Grace, D. M., & Cruwys, T. (2021). Facilitating goals, tasks, and bonds via identity leadership: Understanding the therapeutic working alliance as the outcome of social identity processes. *Group Dynamics: Theory, Research, and Practice*, 25(4), 271–287. https://doi.org/10.1037/gdn0000170

Lee, H., & Choi, H.-S. (2022). Independent self-concept promotes group creativity in a collectivistic cultural context only when the group norm supports collectivism. *Group Dynamics: Theory, Research, and Practice*, 26(1), 71–84. https://doi.org/10.1037/gdn0000129

Lee, M. D., Gluck, K. A., & Walsh, M. M. (2019). Understanding the complexity of simple decisions: Modeling multiple behaviors and switching strategies. *Decision*, 6(4), 335–368. https://doi.org/10.1037/dec0000105

Lee, M. D., Newell, B. R., & Vandekerckhove, J. (2014). Modeling the adaptation of search termination in human decision making. *Decision*, 1(4), 223–251. https://doi.org/10.1037/dec0000019

Leonard, H. S. (2017). A teachable approach to leadership. *Consulting Psychology Journal: Practice and Research, 69*(4), 243–266. https://doi.org/10.1037/cpb0000096

Levenson, A. (2017). Workplace fatigue is a systems problem. *Consulting Psychology Journal: Practice and Research, 69*(2), 130–142. https://doi.org/10.1037/cpb0000091

Levine, S. L., Holding, A. C., Milyavskaya, M., Powers, T. A., & Koestner, R. (2021). Collaborative autonomy: The dynamic relations between personal goal autonomy and perceived autonomy support in emerging adulthood results in positive affect and goal progress. *Motivation Science, 7*(2), 145–152. https://doi.org/10.1037/mot0000209

Levy, N., Harmon-Jones, C., & Harmon-Jones, E. (2018). Dissonance and discomfort: Does a simple cognitive inconsistency evoke a negative affective state? *Motivation Science, 4*(2), 95–108. https://doi.org/10.1037/mot0000079

Li, J., Li, A., Chattopadhyay, P., George, E., & Gupta, V. (2018). Team emotion diversity and performance: The moderating role of social class homogeneity. *Group Dynamics: Theory, Research, and Practice, 22*(2), 76–92. https://doi.org/10.1037/gdn0000083

Liew, S. X., Embrey, J. R., Navarro, D. J., & Newell, B. R. (2022). Comparing anticipation and uncertainty-penalty accounts of noninstrumental information seeking. *Decision.* Advance online publication. https://doi.org/10.1037/dec0000179

Lin, S.-Y., Park, G., Zhou, Q., & Hirst, G. (2022). Two birds, one stone: How altruism can facilitate both individual creativity and prosocial behavior in two different team contexts. *Group Dynamics: Theory, Research, and Practice.* Advance online publication. https://doi.org/10.1037/gdn0000188

Linton, R. K., Critch, S., & Kehoe, E. J. (2018). Role-specific versus cross-role preparation for decision-making teams. *Group Dynamics: Theory, Research, and Practice, 22*(1), 45–60. https://doi.org/10.1037/gdn0000081

Litvinova, A., Herzog, S. M., Kall, A. A., Pleskac, T. J., & Hertwig, R. (2020). How the "wisdom of the inner crowd" can boost accuracy of confidence judgments. *Decision, 7*(3), 183–211. https://doi.org/10.1037/dec0000119

Locke, E. A., & Schattke, K. (2019). Intrinsic and extrinsic motivation: Time for expansion and clarification. *Motivation Science, 5*(4), 277–290. https://doi.org/10.1037/mot0000116

Looney, C. A., & Hardin, A. M. (2020). Beyond Myopia: Wealth Accumulation Mechanisms and Evolving Risk Behaviors. *Decision: A Journal for Research on Judgment and Decision Making, 7*(2), 163–180.

Loyd, D. L., & Amoroso, L. M. (2018). Undermining diversity: Favoritism threat and its effect on advocacy for similar others. *Group Dynamics: Theory, Research, and Practice, 22*(3), 143–155. https://doi.org/10.1037/gdn0000087

Macoveanu, J., Ramsoy, T. Z., Skov, M., Siebner, H. R., & Fosgaard, T. R. (2016). The neural bases of framing effects in social dilemmas. *Journal of Neuroscience, Psychology, and Economics, 9*(1), 14–28. https://doi.org/10.1037/npe0000050

Maier, R. F. (1970). *Problem Solving and Creativity: In Individuals and Groups.* Belmont, CA: Wadsworth Publishing Company, Inc.

Marchiori, D., Di Guida, S., & Erev, I. (2015). Noisy retrieval models of over- and under-sensitivity to rare events. *Decision, 2*(2), 82–106. https://doi.org/10.1037/dec0000023

Maslach, C. (2017). Finding solutions to the problem of burnout. *Consulting Psychology Journal: Practice and Research, 69*(2), 143–152. https://doi.org/10.1037/cpb0000090

Maslow, A. H. (1943). A theory of human motivation. *Psychological Review, 50*(4), 370–396.

Maslow, A. H. (1958). A dynamic theory of human motivation. In Chalmers, S. L. & DeMartino, M. (Ed.) *Understanding Human Motivation,* 26–47. Cleveland, OH: Howard Allen Publishers. https://doi.org/10.1037/11305-004

Mayer, M., & Heck, D. W. (2022). Sequential collaboration: The accuracy of dependent, incremental judgments. *Decision.* Advance online publication. https://doi.org/10.1037/dec0000193

Mayer, R. C., Davis, J. H., & Schoorman, F. D. (1995). An integrative model of organizational trust. *Academy of Management Review, 20*(3), 709–734. www.jstor.org/stable/258792

McGrath, R. E. (2019). Technical report: The VIA Assessment Suite for Adults: Development and initial evaluation (rev. ed.). VIA Institute on Character.

McGuire, W. J. (1968). Theory of the structure of human thought. In Abelson, R. P., Aronson, E., McGuire, W. J, Newcomb, T. M., Rosenberg, M. J., & Tannenbaum, P. H. (Eds.) *Theories of Cognitive Consistency: A Sourcebook,* 140–162. Chicago: Rand McNally and Co.

McLaren, C. D., & Spink, K. S. (2022). Testing boundary conditions in the communication–cohesion relationship in team sport: The case for psychological safety. *Group Dynamics: Theory, Research, and Practice, 26*(1), 12–23. https://doi.org/10.1037/gdn0000161

McLaren, C. D., & Spink, K. S. (2020). Examining the prospective relationship between communication network structure and task cohesion and team performance. *Group Dynamics: Theory, Research, and Practice, 24*(2), 74–87. https://doi.org/10.1037/gdn0000110

Meusburger, P., Funke, J., & Wunder, E. (Eds.) (2009) *Milieus of Creativity: An interdisciplinary approach to spatiality of creativity.* Germany: Springer.

Millroth, P., Nilsson, H., & Juslin, P. (2018). Examining the integrity of evaluations of risky prospects using a single-stimuli design. *Decision, 5*(4), 362–377. https://doi.org/10.1037/dec0000085

Milyavskaya, M., Berkman, E. T., & De Ridder, D. T. D. (2019). The many faces of self-control: Tacit assumptions and recommendations to deal with them. *Motivation Science, 5*(1), 79–85. https://doi.org/10.1037/mot0000108

Mitchell, T. D., & Bommer, W. H. (2018). The interactive effects of motives and task coordination on leadership emergence. *Group Dynamics: Theory, Research, and Practice, 22*(4), 223–235. https://doi.org/10.1037/gdn0000092

Mohammed, S., Alipour, K. K., Martinez, P., Livert, D., & Fitzgerald, D. (2017). Conflict in the kitchen: Temporal diversity and temporal disagreements in chef teams. *Group Dynamics: Theory, Research, and Practice, 21*(1), 1–19. https://doi.org/10.1037/gdn0000058

Moisan, F., ten Brincke, R., Murphy, R. O., & Gonzalez, C. (2018). Not all Prisoner's Dilemma games are equal: Incentives, social preferences, and cooperation. *Decision, 5*(4), 306–322. https://doi.org/10.1037/dec0000079

Müller, R., & Antoni, C. H. (2020). Individual perceptions of shared mental models of information and communication technology (ICT) and virtual team coordination and performance – The moderating role of flexibility in ICT use. *Group Dynamics: Theory, Research, and Practice, 24*(3), 186–200. https://doi.org/10.1037/gdn0000130

Newall, P. W. S., & Love, B. C. (2015). Nudging investors big and small toward better decisions. *Decision, 2*(4), 319–326. https://doi.org/10.1037/dec0000036

Nezu, A. M., Nezu, C. M., & D'Zurilla, T. J. (2007). *Solving Life's Problems: A 5-Step Guide to Enhanced Well-Being.* New York: Springer Publishing Company.

Nickerson, R. S. (1994). The teaching of thinking and problem solving. In Sternberg, R. J. (Ed.) *Thinking and Problem Solving.* San Diego, CA: Academic Press, 409–449.

Novaković, I. Z., Lueger-Schuster, B., Verginer, L., Bakić, H., Ajduković, D., Borges, C., Figueiredo-Braga, M., Javakhishvili, J., Tsiskarishvili, L., Dragan, M., Nagórka, N., Anastassiou-Hadjicharalambous, X., Lioupi, C., & Lotzin, A. (2022). You can't do anything about it, but you can make the best of it: A qualitative analysis of pandemic-related experiences in six European countries. *European Journal of Psychotraumatology*, *13*(1), Article 2065431. https://doi.org/10.1080/20008198.2022.2065431

Nowack, K. (2017). Facilitating successful behavior change: Beyond goal setting to goal flourishing. *Consulting Psychology Journal: Practice and Research*, *69*(3), 153–171. https://doi.org/10.1037/cpb0000088

Nowack, K. (2017). Sleep, emotional intelligence, and interpersonal effectiveness: Natural bedfellows. *Consulting Psychology Journal: Practice and Research*, *69*(2), 66–79. https://doi.org/10.1037/cpb0000077

Nowack, K., & Deal, J. J. (2017). Tired of being fatigued? Introduction to the Special Issue. *Consulting Psychology Journal: Practice and Research*, *69*(2), 63–65. https://doi.org/10.1037/cpb0000093

Nowack, K., & Zak, P. (2020). Empathy enhancing antidotes for interpersonally toxic leaders. *Consulting Psychology Journal: Practice and Research*, *72*(2), 119–133. https://doi.org/10.1037/cpb0000164

Olcaysoy Okten, I., Schneid, E. D., & Moskowitz, G. B. (2019). On the updating of spontaneous impressions. *Journal of Personality and Social Psychology*, *117*(1), 1–25. https://doi.org/10.1037/pspa0000156

Osatuke, K., Yanovsky, B., & Ramsel, D. (2017). Executive coaching: New framework for evaluation. *Consulting Psychology Journal: Practice and Research*, *69*(3), 172–186. https://doi.org/10.1037/cpb0000073

Palaiou, K., & Furnham, A. (2014). Are bosses unique? Personality facet differences between CEOs and staff in five work sectors. *Consulting Psychology Journal: Practice and Research*, *66*(3), 173–196. https://doi.org/10.1037/cpb0000010

Palmer, S., & Whybrow, A. (2017). *What do coaching psychologists and coaches really do? Results from two international surveys*, Invited paper at 7th International Congress of Coaching Psychology October 18, 2017. London.

Panchal, S., Palmer, S., & Green, S. (2019). From positive psychology to the development of positive psychology coaching. In Palmer, S., & Whybrow, A. (Eds.) *Handbook of Coaching Psychology: A guide for practitioners* (2nd edn), 51–67. New York: Routledge.

Parker, P. C., Perry, R. P., Chipperfield, J. G., Hamm, J. M., & Pekrun, R. (2018). An attribution-based motivation treatment for low control students who are bored in online learning environments. *Motivation Science*, *4*(2), 177–184. https://doi.org/10.1037/mot0000081

Pirrone, A., Azab, H., Hayden, B. Y., Stafford, T., & Marshall, J. A. R. (2018). Evidence for the speed–value trade-off: Human and monkey decision making is magnitude sensitive. *Decision*, *5*(2), 129–142. https://doi.org/10.1037/dec0000075

Pleskac, T. J., Yu, S., Hopwood, C., & Liu, T. (2019). Mechanisms of deliberation during preferential choice: Perspectives from computational modeling and individual differences. *Decision*, *6*(1), 77–107. https://doi.org/10.1037/dec0000092

Polya, G. (1985). *How to Solve It: A New Aspect of Mathematical Method*. Princeton University Press.

Posamentier, A. S. (Ed.) (1996). *The Art of Problem Solving: A Resource for the Mathematics Teacher*. Thousand Oaks, CA: Corwin Press.

Pretz, J. E., Naples, A. J., & Sternberg, R. J. (2003). Recognizing, defining, and representing problems. In Davidson, J. E., Sternberg, R. J. (Eds.) *The Psychology of Problem Solving.* New York: Cambridge University Press.

Pugh, M., & Broome, N. (2020). Dialogical coaching: An experiential approach to personal and professional development. *Consulting Psychology Journal: Practice and Research, 72*(3), 223–241. https://doi.org/10.1037/cpb0000162

Pulakos, E., & Kantrowitz, T. (2016). *Choosing Effective Talent Assessments to Strengthen Your Organization.* Alexandria, VA: SHRM Foundation. www.shrm.org/hr-today/trends-and-forecasting/special-reports-and-expert-views/documents/effective-talent-assessments.pdf

Raaheim, K. (1974). *Problem Solving and Intelligence.* Boston: Universitetsforlaget.

Rahn, J., Jaudas, A., & Achtziger, A. (2016). A mind for money: Dynamic mindset effects on smart risk taking. *Journal of Neuroscience, Psychology, and Economics, 9*(3–4), 145–156. https://doi.org/10.1037/npe0000060

Rahn, J., Jaudas, A., & Achtziger, A. (2016). To plan or not to plan – mindset effects on visual attention in decision making. *Journal of Neuroscience, Psychology, and Economics, 9*(2), 109–120. https://doi.org/10.1037/npe0000056

Rank, J., & Gray, D. E. (2017). The role of coaching for relationship satisfaction, self-reflection, and self-esteem: Coachees' self-presentation ability as a moderator. *Consulting Psychology Journal: Practice and Research, 69*(3), 187–208. https://doi.org/10.1037/cpb0000082

Rast, D. E. III, Hogg, M. A., & Giessner, S. R. (2016). Who trusts charismatic leaders who champion change? The role of group identification, membership centrality, and self-uncertainty. *Group Dynamics: Theory, Research, and Practice, 20*(4), 259–275. https://doi.org/10.1037/gdn0000053

Rath, T. (2007). *StrengthsFinder 2.0.* New York: Gallup Press.

Regan, A., Radošić, N., & Lyubomirsky, S. (2022). Experimental effects of social behavior on well-being. *Trends in Cognitive Sciences, 26*(11), 987–998. https://doi.org/10.1016/j.tics.2022.08.006

Regenwetter, M., Cavagnaro, D. R., Popova, A., Guo, Y., Zwilling, C., Lim, S. H., & Stevens, J. R. (2018). Heterogeneity and parsimony in intertemporal choice. *Decision, 5*(2), 63–94. https://doi.org/10.1037/dec0000069

Regenwetter, M., & Robinson, M. M. (2022). Reply to commentaries: Why should we worry about scientific conjunction fallacies? *Decision, 9*(2), 124–130. https://doi.org/10.1037/dec0000176

Regenwetter, M., Robinson, M. M., & Wang, C. (2022). Are you an exception to your favorite decision theory? Behavioral decision research is a linda problem! *Decision, 9*(2), 91–111. https://doi.org/10.1037/dec0000161

Rich, A. S., & Gureckis, T. M. (2018). Exploratory choice reflects the future value of information. *Decision, 5*(3), 177–192. https://doi.org/10.1037/dec0000074

Robertson, S. I. (2001). *Problem Solving.* Philadelphia, PA: Psychology Press.

Rück, F., Dudschig, C., Mackenzie, I. G., Vogt, A., Leuthold, H., & Kaup, B. (2021). The role of predictability during negation processing in truth-value judgment tasks. *Journal of Psycholinguistic Research.* Advance online publication. https://doi.org/10.1007/s10936-021-09804-0

Sackett, E., & Cummings, J. N. (2018). When team members perceive task interdependence differently: Exploring centrality asymmetry and team success. *Group Dynamics: Theory, Research, and Practice, 22*(1), 16–31. https://doi.org/10.1037/gdn0000079

Salamone, J. D., Correa, M., Yohn, S. E., Yang, J.-H., Somerville, M., Rotolo, R. A., & Presby, R. E. (2017). Behavioral activation, effort-based choice, and elasticity of demand for motivational stimuli: Basic and translational neuroscience approaches. *Motivation Science, 3*(3), 208–229. https://doi.org/10.1037/mot0000070

Sana, F., Yan, V. X., Clark, C. M., Bjork, E. L., & Bjork, R. A. (2021). Improving conceptual learning via pretests. *Journal of Experimental Psychology: Applied, 27*(2), 228–236. https://doi.org/10.1037/xap0000322

Sanchez, C., & Dunning, D. (2020). Decision fluency and overconfidence among beginners. *Decision, 7*(3), 225–237. https://doi.org/10.1037/dec0000122

Sawyer, R. K. (2006). *Explaining Creativity: The science of human innovation.* New York: Oxford University Press.

Schaper, M. L., Bayen, U. J., & Hey, C. V. (2022). Delaying metamemory judgments corrects the expectancy illusion in source monitoring: The role of fluency and belief. *Journal of Experimental Psychology: Learning, Memory, and Cognition, 48*(7), 975–1000. https://doi.org/10.1037/xlm0001088

Scheibehenne, B. (2022). Experimenter meets correlator: Comment on Regenwetter et al. (2022). *Decision, 9*(2), 121–123. https://doi.org/10.1037/dec0000169

Schellenberg, B. J. I., & Bailis, D. S. (2018). When decisions are clouded by passion: A look at casino patrons. *Motivation Science, 4*(3), 274–279. https://doi.org/10.1037/mot0000086

Schlinkert, C., & Koole, S. L. (2018). Dealing with life demands: Action-state orientation moderates the relation between demanding conditions and drops in body vitality. *Motivation Science, 4*(2), 118–136. https://doi.org/10.1037/mot0000078

Schlösser, Thomas, Fetchenhauer, Detlef, & Dunning, David. (2016). Trust against all odds? Emotional dynamics in trust behavior. *Decision, 3*(3), 216–230. https://doi.org/10.1037/dec0000048

Seligman, M. (2006). *Learned optimism: How to change your mind and your life.* New York: Vintage Books

Shaughnessy, J. J., Zechmeister, E. B., & Zechmeister, J. S. (2009). *Research Methods in Psychology.* New York: McGraw-Hill

Shavit, Y., Roth, Y., Busemeyer, J., & Teodorescu, K. (2022). Intertemporal decisions from experience versus description: Similarities and differences. *Decision, 9*(2), 131–152. https://doi.org/10.1037/dec0000164

Sheldon, K. M., Goffredi, R., & Schlegel, R. J. (2022). Self-concordant goal-striving as internalized motivation: Benefits beyond person-goal fit. *Motivation Science.* Advance online publication. https://doi.org/10.1037/mot0000277

Shouksmith, G. (1970). *Intelligence, Creativity, and Cognitive Style.* New York: Wiley-Interscience.

Siegling, A. B., Ng-Knight, T., & Petrides, K. V. (2019). Drive: Measurement of a sleeping giant. *Consulting Psychology Journal: Practice and Research, 71*(1), 16–31. https://doi.org/10.1037/cpb0000123

Silvia, P. J., Sizemore, A. J., Tipping, C. J., Perry, L. B., & King, S. F. (2018). Get going! Self-focused attention and sensitivity to action and inaction effort primes. *Motivation Science, 4*(2), 109–117. https://doi.org/10.1037/mot0000077

Smithson, M., & Shou, Y. (2021). How big is (sample) space? Judgment and decision making with unknown states and outcomes. *Decision, 8*(4), 237–256. https://doi.org/10.1037/dec0000154

Sokolowska, J., Michalaszek, A., & Gugala, I. (2021). The Perceived Risk-Value Relation and Models of Preferences. *Decision: A Journal for Research on Judgment and Decision Making, 8*(4), 327–345.

Stavros, J., & Torres, C. (2021). *Conversations Worth Having: Using Appreciative Inquiry to Fuel Productive and Meaningful Engagement*. Oakland, CA: Berrett-Koehler Publishers, Inc.

Stein, S. S., & Book, H. E. (2011). *The EQ Edge: Emotional intelligence and your success* (3rd edn). Mississauga, ON: John Wiley & Sons.

Steiner, M. D., Seitz, F. I., & Frey, R. (2021). Through the window of my mind: Mapping information integration and the cognitive representations underlying self-reported risk preference. *Decision, 8*(2), 97–122. https://doi.org/10.1037/dec0000127

Sternberg, R. J. (2007). *Wisdom, Intelligence, and Creativity Synthesized*. New York: Cambridge University Press.

Stevenson, M. K. (2019). Temporal discounting and context: Discounting weights for gains and losses presented in isolation and in combination. *Decision, 6*(3), 261–276. https://doi.org/10.1037/dec0000099

Sverdrup, T. E., Schei, V., & Tjølsen, Ø. A. (2017). Expecting the unexpected: Using team charters to handle disruptions and facilitate team performance. *Group Dynamics: Theory, Research, and Practice, 21*(1), 53–59. https://doi.org/10.1037/gdn0000059

Svetieva, E., Clerkin, C., & Ruderman, M. N. (2017). Can't sleep, won't sleep: Exploring leaders' sleep patterns, problems, and attitudes. *Consulting Psychology Journal: Practice and Research, 69*(2), 80–97. https://doi.org/10.1037/cpb0000092

Tabibnia, G., & Radecki, D. (2018). Resilience training that can change the brain. *Consulting Psychology Journal: Practice and Research, 70*(1), 59–88. https://doi.org/10.1037/cpb0000110

Thommes, M. S., & Uitdewilligen, S. (2019). Healthy suspicion: The value of low swift trust for information processing and performance of temporary teams. *Group Dynamics: Theory, Research, and Practice, 23*(2), 124–139. https://doi.org/10.1037/gdn0000102

Tomyn, A. J. (2017). Hadley Cantril: A pioneer in public opinion research. *Applied Research Quality Life, 12*, 1033–1034. https://doi.org/10.1007/s11482-017-9569-9

Topa, G., & Herrador-Alcaide, T. (2016). Procrastination and financial planning for retirement: A moderated mediation analysis. *Journal of Neuroscience, Psychology, and Economics, 9*(3–4), 169–181. https://doi.org/10.1037/npe0000065

Torrance, E. P., & Myers, R. E. (1972) *Creative Learning and Teaching*. New York: Dodd, Mead, & Company.

Tuckman, B. W. (1965). Developmental sequence in small groups. *Psychological Bulletin, 63*(6), 384–399. https://doi.org/10.1037/h0022100

Uddenberg, S., & Shim, W. M. (2015). Seeing the world through target-tinted glasses: Positive mood broadens perceptual tuning. *Emotion, 15*(3), 319–328. https://doi.org/10.1037/emo0000029

Unger-Aviram, E., Zeigler-Hill, V., Barina, M., & Besser, A. (2018). Narcissism, collective efficacy, and satisfaction in self-managed teams: The moderating role of team goal orientation. *Group Dynamics: Theory, Research, and Practice, 22*(3), 172–186. https://doi.org/10.1037/gdn0000089

Uziel, L., Baumeister, R. F., & Alquist, J. L. (2021). What makes people want more self-control: A duo of deficiency and necessity. *Motivation Science, 7*(3), 242–251. https://doi.org/10.1037/mot0000213

Valshtein, T. J., & Seta, C. E. (2019). Behavior-goal consistency and the role of anticipated and retrospective regret in self-regulation. *Motivation Science, 5*(1), 35–51. https://doi.org/10.1037/mot0000101

Van Gestel, L. C., Adriaanse, M. A., & De Ridder, D. T. D. (2021). Motivated by default – How nudges facilitate people to act in line with their motivation. *Motivation Science, 7*(3), 319–333. https://doi.org/10.1037/mot0000230

Van Oosten, E. B., McBride-Walker, S. M., & Taylor, S. N. (2019). Investing in what matters: The impact of emotional and social competency development and executive coaching on leader outcomes. *Consulting Psychology Journal: Practice and Research, 71*(4), 249–269. https://doi.org/10.1037/cpb0000141

van Swol, L. M., Chang, C.-T., & Gong, Z. (2022). The benefits of advice from outgroup members on decision accuracy and bias reduction. *Decision.* Advance online publication. https://doi.org/10.1037/dec0000173

Vandaveer, V. V., Lowman, R. L., Pearlman, K., & Brannick, J. P. (2016). A practice analysis of coaching psychology: Toward a foundational competency model. *Consulting Psychology Journal: Practice and Research, 68*(2), 118–142. https://doi.org/10.1037/cpb0000057

Vohs, K. D., Baumeister, R. F., Schmeichel, B. J., Twenge, J. M., Nelson, N. M., & Tice, D. M. (2014). Making choices impairs subsequent self-control: A limited-resource account of decision making, self-regulation, and active initiative. *Motivation Science, 1*(S), 19–42. https://doi.org/10.1037/2333-8113.1.S.19

von Treuer, K., McLeod, J., Fuller-Tyszkiewicz, M., & Scott, G. (2018). Determining the components of cohesion using the repertory grid technique. *Group Dynamics: Theory, Research, and Practice, 22*(2), 108–128. https://doi.org/10.1037/gdn0000085

Vonasch, A. J., Vohs, K. D., Pocheptsova Ghosh, A., & Baumeister, R. F. (2017). Ego depletion induces mental passivity: Behavioral effects beyond impulse control. *Motivation Science, 3*(4), 321–336. https://doi.org/10.1037/mot0000058

Wagner, R., & Muller, G. (2009). *Power of 2: How to Make the Most of Your Partnerships at Work and in Life.* New York: Gallup Press.

Walker, D., Smith, K. A., & Vul, E. (2022). Reconsidering the "bias" in "the correspondence bias." *Decision, 9*(3), 263–284. https://doi.org/10.1037/dec0000180

Wallace, D. M., & Hinsz, V. B. (2019). A social judgment analysis of information processing in groups: Capacity and consistency in information processing impacts group judgment. *Group Dynamics: Theory, Research, and Practice, 23*(3–4), 143–155. https://doi.org/10.1037/gdn0000107

Wallin, A., Swait, J., & Marley, A. A. J. (2018). Not just noise: A goal pursuit interpretation of stochastic choice. *Decision, 5*(4), 253–271. https://doi.org/10.1037/dec0000077

Wallis, A., Robertson, J., Bloore, R. A., & Jose, P. E. (2021). Differences and similarities between leaders and nonleaders on psychological distress, well-being, and challenges at work. *Consulting Psychology Journal: Practice and Research, 73*(4), 325–348. https://doi.org/10.1037/cpb0000214

Walsh, J. A., & Sattes, B. D. (2010). *Leading Through Quality Questioning: Creating Capacity, Commitment, and Community.* Thousand Oaks, CA: Corwin.

Walsh, J. A., & Sattes, B. D. (2015). *Questioning for Classroom Discussion.* Alexandria, VA: ASCD.

Wei, X., Liu, Y., & Allen, N. J. (2016). Measuring team emotional intelligence: A multimethod comparison. *Group Dynamics: Theory, Research, and Practice, 20*(1), 34–50. https://doi.org/10.1037/gdn0000039

Weinert, F. E., & Kluwe, R. H. (Eds.) (1987). *Metacognition, motivation, and understanding.* Hillsdale, NJ: Lawrence Erlbaum Associates, Publishers.

Weisberg, R. W. (1999). Creativity and knowledge: A challenge to theories. In Sternberg, R. J. (Ed.) *Handbook of Creativity,* 226–250. New York: Cambridge University Press.

Weisberg, R. W. (2006). *Creativity: Understanding Innovation in Problem Solving, Science, Invention, and the Arts.* Hoboken, NJ: John Wiley & Sons.

Welch, D., Grossaint, K., Reid, K., & Walker, C. (2014). Strengths-based leadership development: Insights from expert coaches. *Consulting Psychology Journal: Practice and Research*, 66(1), 20–37. https://doi.org/10.1037/cpb0000002

White, R. P. (2017). Toward a deeper understanding of the role of trusted leadership advisor, and knowing if you are ready for it. *Consulting Psychology Journal: Practice and Research*, 69(1), 32–35. https://doi.org/10.1037/cpb0000084

Wickman, G. (2011). *Traction: Get a Grip on Your Business* Expanded Edition. Dallas, TX: BenBella.

Wilcox, E. W. (1913). *'Tis the set of the Sail: One ship sails east.* www.poemist.com/ella-wheeler-wilcox/tis-the-set-of-the-sail-or-one-ship-sails-east accessed April 26, 2023.

Williams, H., Palmer, S., & Gyllensten, K. (2019). Stress, resilience, health and wellbeing coaching. In Palmer, S., & Whybrow, A. (Eds.) *Handbook of Coaching Psychology: A Guide for Practitioners* (2nd edn), 395–409. New York: Routledge.

Wood, D., Lowman, G. H., Armstrong, B. F. III, & Harms, P. D. (2022). Using retest-adjusted correlations as indicators of the semantic similarity of items. *Journal of Personality and Social Psychology.* Advance online publication. https://doi.org/10.1037/pspp0000441

Worthy, D. A., Otto, A. R., Doll, B. B., Byrne, K. A., & Maddox, W. T. (2015). Older adults are highly responsive to recent events during decision-making. *Decision, 2*(1), 27–38. https://doi.org/10.1037/dec0000018

Yan, V. X., Bjork, E. L., & Bjork, R. A. (2016). On the difficulty of mending metacognitive illusions: A priori theories, fluency effects, and misattributions of the interleaving benefit. *Journal of Experimental Psychology: General, 145*(7), 918–933. https://doi.org/10.1037/xge0000177

Yan, V. X., Soderstrom, N. C., Seneviratna, G. S., Bjork, E. L., & Bjork, R. A. (2017). How should exemplars be sequenced in inductive learning? Empirical evidence versus learners' opinions. *Journal of Experimental Psychology: Applied, 23*(4), 403–416. https://doi.org/10.1037/xap0000139

Yoerger, M., Crowe, J., & Allen, J. A. (2015). Participate or else!: The effect of participation in decision-making in meetings on employee engagement. *Consulting Psychology Journal: Practice and Research, 67*(1), 65–80. https://doi.org/10.1037/cpb0000029

Yost, P. R., Yoder, M. P., Chung, H. H., & Voetmann, K. R. (2015). Narratives at work: Story arcs, themes, voice, and lessons that shape organizational life. *Consulting Psychology Journal: Practice and Research, 67*(3), 163–188. https://doi.org/10.1037/cpb0000043

Yu, C. S.-P., McBeath, M. K., & Glenberg, A. M. (2021). The gleam-glum effect:/i:/versus/λ/ phonemes generically carry emotional valence. *Journal of Experimental Psychology: Learning, Memory, and Cognition, 47*(7), 1173–1185. https://doi.org/10.1037/xlm0001017

Zeitz, P. (1999). *The Art and Craft of Problem Solving.* Hoboken, NJ: John Wiley & Sons, Inc.

Index

References to figures appear in *italic* type; and those in **bold** type refer to tables.

Printed in the United States
by Baker & Taylor Publisher Services